my father
my friend

my father
my friend

lessons on life and love

DAVID CHADWICK

HENDRICKSON
PUBLISHERS

© 2002 by Hendrickson Publishers, Inc.
P. O. Box 3473
Peabody, Massachusetts 01961–3473

Printed in the United States of America

First Printing—April 2002

Library of Congress Cataloging-in-Publication Data

Chadwick, David.
    My father, my friend : lessons on life and love / by David Chadwick.
       p. cm.
    ISBN 1-56563-732-1 (hardcover : alk. paper)
    1. Fathers—Religious life. 2. Christian men—Religious life. I. Title.
    BV4529.17 .C43 2002
    248.4—dc21
                      2002001483

"I'm pleased David has taken the time to share the positive impact his father has had upon his life. I've known them both since 1967 when I was recruiting David as a scholar-athlete at the University of North Carolina. David's deep love and respect for his father were obvious from the beginning. I hope the truths David gleaned about life from his father can now help many others learn the powerful, positive impact fathers can and should have on their own children and all members of society."

> — Coach Dean Smith, former Head Basketball
> Coach, the University of North Carolina

"In our contemporary era of absent fathers, both physically and emotionally, and confused fathers, both spiritually and culturally, David's book about his dad breaks like the dawn upon a benighted world. With candor and conviction David enlightens and challenges us. With refreshing insight David reorients us to the timeless truths about the profound impact of fatherly love and limits. Never before have the leadership and example of Christian fathers been more needed. Never before have the basic principles of fatherhood been more clearly defined or more warmly illustrated. David Chadwick's dad has been an inspiration to his son and now is to us. May his tribe increase."

> — Sid Bradley, Dean of Gordon-Conwell
> Theological Seminary, Charlotte

"Just what America needs—a good dose of common sense!"

> — Sue Myrick, U.S. House of Representatives

"The difference between right and wrong has never been more evident than it is now. David Chadwick has correctly refocused our attention on the rightness of strong two-parent families. He reminds us of a father's obligation to love his wife and their call to demonstrate to their children how love and respect break down life's most difficult barriers. This is a timely, appropriate, and much needed reminder of how we should treat each other. It's a great read for everyone, especially dads."

— Robin Hayes, U.S. House of Representatives

"David Chadwick's excellent book provides refreshing nuggets of wisdom that will be enjoyed by young and old. In a world too often dominated by bad news, it is a wonderful testimony that positive role models still exist. Chadwick' s book is destined to provide hope and encouragement to countless readers."

— Dr. Robert Schuller, Pastor of the Crystal Cathedral

"Having been involved in intercollegiate athletics for the past three decades, I've certainly seen the negative impact of fatherless homes in America. We should do anything and everything we can to encourage fathers to become positive role models for their children. Therefore, it is my pleasure to endorse this book about David's dad. Children today don't need more things from their fathers, they need their fathers. The principles for life, parenting, family, and relationships that are outlined here will be valuable for anyone who desires to know how to be a better father or to discover what a positive father can mean in our lives. The principles aren't new, but they are basic for the survival of the family. My hope is we'll not only read about them in David and Howard Chadwick's lives, but also actually apply them. We'll all be better because of it."

— John Swofford, Commissioner of the Atlantic Coast Conference

"David's book about his father reminded me of the many crucial points of wisdom my own dad gave me throughout my life. Thanks, David. Although my dad passed away in 1995, your book brought me even closer to him and to God."

— Pat McCrory, Mayor of Charlotte, North Carolina

"Being the father of four children, I know the importance firsthand of being a good father. I am thankful David has taken the time to write this timely and valuable book."

— P. J. Brown of the Charlotte Hornets

"As a former athlete, I truly believe the one trophy more of us need to talk about is the one we all should want on our mantles: a picture of our families. In the end, the success and stability of our children are far more important than any personal success we've been able to achieve. Therefore, it's my privilege to recommend this book by my friend David Chadwick. Knowing David for almost thirty years, it's easy to see how some wonderful people have had a powerful impact on his life. I know Coach Dean Smith is one of these people, as he has been in my life. Likewise, it's also easy to see how much David's dad has meant to him. Therefore, I sincerely hope that many people will read this book and learn what is most important in life. The principles of positive fathering outlined here will help us all achieve the most important trophy of all: a picture of a healthy, together, loving family guided by the hands of a loving father."

— Mitch Kupchak, General Manager of the Los Angeles Lakers

Dedicated to my mom, Helen Chadwick,
without whom Howard Chadwick
could never have been the great dad he is.

Table of Contents

Part One: Marriage 1

The best gift you can give your kids is to love their
mother. 3

What a heaven of a lot you've missed. 5

That's the woman I love you're talking to! 9

I simply love her. 11

It's easy to leave your spouse. It's very difficult to
leave your best friend! 14

Love is something you do. 16

You need some space in your togetherness. 18

The closer two people become, the more they bump. 21

Part Two: Parenting 25

I can always buy a new car, but I can't buy a new you. 27

You've never lied to me before, and I believe you now. 31

Don't worry what people are thinking about you.
They're not thinking about you at all. They are
too busy thinking about themselves. 34

Kids spell love T-I-M-E. 36

Howard needs me. 41

You're always a parent, no matter what age they are. 45

If a man doesn't have his word, he has nothing. 48

Are you OK? Please come here.   51

It's because I love you that I am going to discipline you.   56

I trust you. I don't trust your hormones.   58

It was just a dress rehearsal before the main
        performance.   60

I am proud of you, Son.   63

You are who you are, not what you do   66

Did you do your best?   68

God bless you!   71

Part Three: Personal Counsel   75

My father just died.   77

Friends are like elevators. They either take you up
        or they bring you down.   79

Remember whose and who you are.   81

Reasonable people know somewhere there must be
        a ceiling.   83

When you're late, you're stealing other people's time.   85

There is a huge difference between your wants and
        needs.   87

The most important shot is the next one.   90

Avoid the snare to compare.   92

With every right, there is a responsibility.   94

I'm sorry. I was simply wrong.   96

It had to be your decision.   98

Keep an open mind, but don't let your brains fall out.   100

A good carpenter doesn't blame his tools.   103

Shoot for the stars. You may only arrive at the moon,
        but you've never been to the moon before.   106

Table of Contents

Don't listen too closely when people jeer or cheer.   108

Always remember to diet and exercise.   110

The enemy of the best is the good.   112

Tears are God's way of keeping a head from becoming big.   114

Never retire. Just re-fire.   117

If the sun comes up, there's always hope.   119

Part Four: Relationships   123

Give it the test of time.   125

Get so close he can't kick you.   127

I try to understand their side.   129

They'll need a new pastor.   133

Beware of dream killers.   136

The more you stir manure, the more it stinks.   138

Dogs only bark at moving cars.   141

Don't look at what you've lost but what you've got left.   144

The grass may seem greener on the other side, but it still needs to be mowed.   146

Choose your battles wisely.   148

Be responsible, but don't take responsibility.   150

Always treat people the right way. You never know when you may need them to help you!   152

Part Five: Faith   157

I just knew he loved me.   159

I can still see her dancing around the room.   162

God always tests a calling.   165

God never looks at who you are, but who you can
    become.   168

Faith is not taught but caught.   170

Adversity is life's university.   173

My God, in all his loving kindness, has met me at
    every corner.   176

We know who waits for us on the other side.   179

In you, Dad, I see the face of God my eternal Father.   181

Epilogue   183

Marriage

*"The best gift you can give your
kids is to love their mother."*

I had waited a relatively long time for the right person to
marry. But when she came, well, as they say, "It was all over
but the shouting."

Marilynn and I had a whirlwind courtship. It was very intense. We both admit we fell in love on the first date and talked
marriage within the first month. Five months later we were engaged. Four months after that we celebrated our wedding. We
certainly don't counsel couples to do similarly; yet, here we are
twenty-plus years later and still going strong!

On the night before the wedding, I was feeling some nostal-
gia. I was with my dad. He was reflecting with me over his many
years of marriage with Mom. I shared with him my desire one
day to have children.

On a whim I asked, "Dad, give me one sound piece of
parenting advice for my kids I hope to have one day."

He leaned back in his chair and thought a few moments. Finally, he said, "Son, here is the absolute best parenting counsel

I can give you. The best gift you can give your kids is to love their mother."

One time Marilynn and I were having one of those moments filled with angst between us. The tension filled the room like a fog. Everyone in the house, especially our three children, felt it. Finally, one of them, without saying a word, approached us, took the hand of one and then the other, and fastened them together with his hand. He then pulled us together. We hugged. Believe me, we didn't feel like hugging one another. What happened next was extraordinary. He put his little arms around us. We couldn't help but put our arms around one another.

Calm entered our home. I remembered how children need security. When there is tension between Mom and Dad, there is tension in the home. When Mom and Dad kiss or embrace in their presence, they may be saying "Yuck" on the outside, but on the inside they are yelling, "Go for it, Dad. Yeah, Mom!"

I sometimes need to be reminded. Often I'm simply hardheaded and hardhearted and don't heed perhaps the wisest parenting principle ever given to me.

In case you've never heard it, or perhaps you've just forgotten—whatever the reason—let my Dad help parent your children, as he has mine, with some sage counsel from the night before my wedding:

"The best gift you can give your kids is to love their mother."

"What a heaven of a lot you've missed."

M uch of our society is commitment-phobic. People, for a variety of reasons, don't want to make commitments, especially in marriage. I'm increasingly running into both males and females (honestly, more males than females) who are reluctant to make lifelong commitments in marriage.

I think that's sad, and here's why: Mom and Dad have been married almost sixty years! Yep, you heard correctly, sixty years. It seems like they are anachronistic, a dying breed.

I hope not. Call me an incurable romantic if you want, but I still think a long, monogamous marriage is heaven's best idea. I see it in Mom and Dad's lives. I want it for myself.

I'll never forget when Dad made this truth real for me. He came home from his work as a pastor. His brow was furrowed. His eyes squinted from a slight headache.

I asked what was wrong. He shrugged and simply said, "A long day . . . and a crazy counseling session to end it!"

I naturally asked for details. He hesitated for a moment, probably not wanting to relive the stress through which he had already gone. Then he answered, "He is a relatively well-known man in the community. He came to me because his life is a mess. He has gone through several marriages and is reputed to have experienced many different extramarital indiscretions. He is miserable inside. He came to me for help and advice."

There was a moment of silence.

"What did you say to him?" I asked.

"Well," Dad continued, "I told him that the best marriages and most meaningful relationships in the world are when a man and woman commit their hearts, souls, and minds together in a unified, monogamous, life-long commitment. I told him sex was intended by God to be used solely within the confines of this committed relationship. I told him that sex was like glue. When we rightly use it as God intended, it cements a relationship. I told him that there is nothing more beautiful than this commitment within marriage. It deepens love and respect and only increases our joy and happiness as the years go by."

"How did he respond to your beliefs?" I asked.

Dad chuckled, still stewing over the man's words.

"He asked me in stark disbelief, 'You mean to tell me that you've been faithful to only one woman for all the years of your married life?' I told him that's exactly what I was saying."

"How did he respond to that?" I asked.

"He looked at me like I was from Mars. Then he finally said, 'Man, what a hell of a lot you've missed in life!'"

"Well," I asked, "how did you respond to that?"

"I simply shrugged my shoulders. Then I told him what a heaven of a lot he had missed. Then he left my office as miserable as he had entered."

I love to tell this story to this day. I think Dad does too. Here he is, on the other side of sixty years of marriage, and I'm certain he has lived out this truth.

Now, I have a weekly radio program on WBT, Charlotte's largest secular station. It attempts to interpret contemporary issues through the lenses of faith and values. Occasionally, the program director asks me to do live talk radio when a faith issue confronts the culture. He did so when the Jesse Jackson scandal revealing the birth of his illegitimate child hit the news. He asked me to answer calls for several hours as people vented their views.

During the program, I told this story about Dad. Most people responded very positively. However, one particularly acerbic caller said, "I don't believe this for a moment. All you preacher-types are the same. You're all spouting pious phrases from your pulpits and cheating on the side."

He pushed my button. I am absolutely certain of my faithfulness to Marilynn. Moreover, I was even more certain Dad had been faithful to Mom for sixty years! I let the caller have it (of course with great love!). Sorry, folks. I guess we all have our limits.

Their marriage isn't perfect. Not one marriage is. However, it is filled with qualities such as mutual respect and care. It's more and more rooted in unconditional love. I can only hope one day to communicate with Marilynn with such depth and substance.

As I presently watch Dad hold Mom's had as she wavers while walking, as I see her pat his hand while eating, as I see two lives that are truly one—at least partly because of fidelity—well, probably the best way I can describe it is:

Committed, or even better,

Heavenly.

"That's the woman I love you're talking to!"

W hen I look at Mom's and Dad's marriage, I've always respected their apparent oneness together. The two really have become one!

I'm certain they've had to work at it through the years. I'm equally certain it's been a process that has developed. This was evidenced at different times in their marriage when they had to make difficult life choices. For example, when Dad was trying to decide whether to accept a particular calling that not only would move us to another church in another city, but also included changing denominations, he could not sleep at nights. He was speaking in another city and had to ride the train overnight. During a restless, fitful night, God spoke to his heart, and he knew what he was supposed to do.

Mom met him at the train station the next morning. When he stepped off the train, Mom simply looked into his eyes and knew the decision had been made. In fact, the same peace had entered her heart the night before.

Some experts talk about how identical twins separated at birth enjoy an emotional, relational bond even though separated by thousands of miles. Stories are told how even though they have never met, suddenly, without warning, one will experience pain on the East Coast and the other on the West Coast will experience the exact same pain. It's a mysterious union, the oneness a great marriage is supposed to experience.

Dad used to tell us when we were kids, "If you ever talk negatively to your mom, realize at that moment you are also talking to me."

These were mere words until one evening at dinner. We were all sitting around the table, engaging in family small talk. I can't remember exactly what happened, but the conversation became a bit more heated. Mom said something to correct Howard, my older brother. He shot back something that was anything but respectful.

Dad shot out of his chair toward Howard, and the intensity of his actions surprised us all. But I'll never forget his words.

"I'll have you know that's the woman I love you're talking to."

He made his point. If you talk to Mom disrespectfully, you may as well be talking to him.

I could tell Mom felt relieved, indeed protected.

They were one flesh, one life together.

We kids needed to remember that truth.

Personally, I've never forgotten it.

"I simply love her."

＊

I t happened around ten years ago. Mom had just undergone successful knee surgery. The doctors had replaced a deteriorated knee.

It was not immediately perceptible. However, everyone in the family, especially Dad, began to notice it. She first started misplacing things and forgetting where she had left them. Then you would tell her things, and she would forget. As the years have passed, the problem has been exacerbated. In their twilight years, I have watched my dad care for the woman he dearly loves without complaint.

We don't know the exact diagnosis. Does it really matter?

It has been especially difficult for Dad. Sometimes they can't even carry on a conversation. She can remember vividly what happened fifty years ago in her family but can't remember what happened three minutes ago. Spiritually, it's difficult. Their oneness of faith is challenged as, for example, prayer and worship can't be experienced in the depth known before. Physically, it's challenging. Dad has been forced to assume the role of caregiver and chore-doer. He's now in his eighties, and the emotional, spiritual, and physical strength simply aren't there anymore.

One particular evening, Mom was especially incoherent. She repeated herself over and over again. (We've learned to appreciate the moments when she is lucid!) Dad became increasingly irritable, as we all did. Dad is not a plaster saint without flaws. Like all of us, he has his limits.

When she left the room, Dad started to cry. I knew what was going on. He was grieving over the loss of what he had known. He was also staring into the dark, mysterious future, not knowing what was facing him or her.

In a startling moment of stupidity or insensitivity, I carelessly asked Dad, "Do you ever think about leaving her?"

He looked at me as if I were from Mars. At that moment, he probably didn't think he had fathered me!

"Of course not!"

Continuing on my track of absolute stupidity, I asked "Why? Dad, she is not the person you married."

Without blinking, he stiffened. He quietly yet firmly responded, "Because I love her." Then, as if for emphasis, he repeated those powerful words, "Because I love her."

The next moments of silence yelled in my ears. Then he broke the silence. This was a life lesson that needed to be learned. I sensed he needed to speak.

"You know, Son," he said, "I don't know where my generation failed to teach your generation about true love. But we did. Love in marriage isn't this spontaneous feeling portrayed by Hollywood that, when it's gone, so is love. Love in marriage isn't only until you change and become a different person than the person I married.

"The vows I took on that wedding day years ago said 'for better or worse.' This is now worse. We said to one another we were committed to one another 'in sickness and in health.' This is sickness.

"Has she changed? Yes. But so have I. Do I still feel love for her? Of course I do. But in a deeper, richer way than Hollywood could ever understand. We have more than fifty years of shared life. We've experienced pain, troubles, and anguish of heart together. We've shouted for joy and celebrated together. We've birthed three kids together. Our lives are intertwined. The love in our souls is melted together in ways I can't explain to you.

"Leave her?" he concluded. "I may as well leave myself. I could never leave her. I not only made a vow before God, family, and friends never to do so, but more importantly, I love her. I simply love her."

I'm beginning to understand, Dad, after twenty-plus years of my own marriage. I really am.

I'm sorry for my insensitivity and stupidity that night. I should have known better. Thanks for redeeming it. Thanks for teaching me a significant life lesson. It is a lesson many need to learn in this me-centered culture in which we live.

Thanks for teaching me what love really is.

"It's easy to leave your spouse. It's very difficult to leave your best friend."

■

I am certain one of Dad's disappointments in life has been his inability to enjoy these twilight years with Mom. They had dreams of travelling together, enjoying their grandchildren together, seeing life reach its myriad positive zeniths together.

However, time, aging, and memory lapses have robbed them of this potential twilight bliss. Mom's momentary lucidity shows what could have been but will never be.

Interestingly, on several occasions, I've asked, "Really, she's your best friend?"

He always responds, "Yes. There's no one else with whom I'd rather spend time. Memories forge our friendship. Yes, Son, she's my best friend."

Which may be the primary reason they're still together after sixty-plus years of marriage. After all, as Dad shared with me once:

"It's easy to leave your spouse. It's very difficult to leave your best friend."

Part One: Marriage

Guess what? My wife, Marilynn, is my best friend. We're twenty years into our marriage.

Bet you it lasts into our sixtieth and beyond! I have no doubt about it.

Why?

Because I could never leave my best friend.

Never!

"Love is something you do."

O ver the past few years, it has been exceedingly difficult to watch Dad exert so much physical energy in caring for Mom. In their previous years of marriage, Mom took care of the house and meals; Dad worked in his calling and supplied the money so the home could run in an orderly fashion.

However, as Mom's mental and physical capacities have become increasingly limited, Dad has been forced to assume the entire responsibility. He not only cooks, but also needs to make sure Mom eats. She has withered from a finely-figured woman to an emaciated figure who barely resembles our memories of her. He cleans the house, tries to make sure the yard is properly managed, and oversees the books.

For years Dad has taught that, from God's viewpoint, one of the purposes of suffering is to conform us to the servant-image of Jesus. Pain often forces us to realize that we actually control little in life and then choose to give our lives to others, which, ultimately, is God's plan for us all.

Now I see Dad living what he taught us. No longer is he driven to success for personal gain. He is serving my mom with the love of Jesus. No longer does he care about the siren songs of worldly gain. He is serving my mom with the love of Jesus. No longer do things of impermanent value lure his heart. He is serving my mom with the love of Jesus.

I see God shaping the inward quality of Dad's heart. Yes, there seems to be purpose even in this suffering.

I recently asked Dad what he thought God might be doing in all this. I questioned him why God might be allowing all this to happen to him.

His answer forces us all to pause.

He simply said, "I think God is teaching me that love is something I do, not just something I feel."

In a culture that glamorizes love as something related to feelings of the moment, I think Dad exposes the lie.

Love is something we do. And God's purpose is for it to last for a lifetime.

This one is a difficult lesson to learn, Dad, but I'm trying.

And keep trying until I go home to meet perfect love, my Creator.

"You need some space in your togetherness."

D ad loves sports. Mom could care less, unless I was play-ing. Then she became a fanatic. I'll never forget my alma mater Orlando Boone High School playing Bishop Moore, a local Catholic School.

With just a few seconds left, the score was tied. I looked into the stands and saw Mom rocking back and forth, hands clasped, head bowed, praying up a storm. I don't know why, but I glanced to the Bishop Moore side of court. Amazingly, three Catholic nuns sat rocking back and forth, hands clasped, heads bowed, praying up a storm.

"Uh, oh," I though, as my head darted from one side to the other. "It's three against one. We don't have a chance!" My team won on a last-second shot. But I seriously doubt if the Al-mighty caused it!

Anyway, I've learned, in watching Mom's and Dad's mar-riage, that you don't have to have everything in common to have a successful marriage. While Dad was watching sports,

Mom might be in the bedroom reading. Or sometimes she'd stay in the TV room, knitting, just to be near Dad.

Once Dad shared with me why this worked for them. "Son," he said, "a good marriage is like two columns holding up a roof. If they're too close together, the building collapses. If there's the right space between them, they are together, strong enough to hold up the house."

"In other words," he concluded, "as Gibran said, 'there needs to be space in your togetherness.'"

One of the major issues in martial problems is unrealistic expectations of the other. We set ourselves up for failure when the other doesn't live up to our expectations, which will happen often!

Perhaps the only way to solve this potential problem is to accept the reality that columns need to be a bit apart for full strength to occur. Couples need to realize that true strength comes when there's some space in your togetherness.

You do need to have some things you enjoy doing together, but not everything.

As the French say, "Vive la différence."

Oh, yes, I love sports. I love to play and watch all kinds of sports.

Marilynn, my beloved, could care less. She does watch our kids play. (I think she, too, prays during the games, but don't tell her I said so!)

We deeply love each other. We're very, very close; we're best friends. We do enjoy doing things together: a walk on the beach, a good movie (no violence or gratuitous sex, please), a wonderful, intimate meal out (alone, no kids, please), a warm fire on a cool, crisp night, just being, holding hands. . . .

We love being together and, sometimes, also love being apart. Because the space encourages intimacy when we're together!

Another lesson from a dad whose marriage is sixty years young.

You need some space in your togetherness.

*"The closer two people become,
the more they bump."*

▨

I thought I'd never hear Dad utter these words. I could tell work was really getting to him. Only those in ministry can understand its pressures and expectations. At any time, a minister must be visionary leader, counselor, administrator, financier, motivator, staff-overseer, and personal caregiver, while always being available!

One evening, he and Mom were snipping at one another. I noticed that it happened from time to time, but they always made up, and the crisis would pass. As Dad once said to me, "The closer two people become, the more they bump!" They were extremely close and occasionally bumped.

But this time the bumping seemed to be more intense. One evening, while I was a teenager, I was upstairs in my bedroom. The conversation between my parents downstairs became a bit more intense, a bit louder with every exchange. Eventually, their voices were quite loud, and I could hear every word. Mom was concerned about Dad's load and his lack of involvement with her and the kids. He felt overloaded, trapped. He felt she was being insensitive.

Then I heard words from his mouth I thought I'd never hear: "I must leave."

I inched my way down the stairs and peeked around the corner into his bedroom. I couldn't believe my ears that I'd heard him threaten to leave. I *really* couldn't believe my eyes when I saw him packing his bags to leave.

Please picture the scene with me: Mom is in the living room crying. Dad is packing his bags to leave to go to I don't know where. Moreover, a gawky teenager is staring, incredulous, at the man he loves and respects.

"Dad," I stammered, "what are you doing?"

He froze in his tracks as he suddenly realized I had not only heard the argument but was a witness to his actions. Like a statue, he remained frozen in the posture of placing another shirt in his suitcase. Then he fell to his knees and started crying like a baby.

I don't remember exactly how long it took. Nevertheless, finally, trying to control his sobs, he went into the living room and observed his red-eyed wife. Meekly, quietly, he uttered those words so difficult to say to one with whom we've argued: "I'm sorry. Please forgive me. Let's talk."

Mom nodded affirmatively, not saying a word. Dad went and sat next to her. Their hands slowly touched. Healing began.

I inwardly said, "Whew!"

As traumatic as that experience was, I'm very grateful it occurred. First, I saw my parents as real people. I saw they had marital struggles, as all couples do. Second, in my own marriage, when conflict occurs, it doesn't surprise me. I know it's normal. Plus, I know it can eventually be overcome and can lead a couple to a greater intimacy.

Some children grow up in homes with no apparent conflict. Either the parents have passive personalities and never have conflict (something I can't imagine but admit is possible, but not probable), or there is conflict in the home, but the kids never see it.

The second possibility scares me. Why? Because most normal, healthy relationships have conflict. Indeed, in my opinion, it's inevitable for conflict to occur in marriage.

Therefore, what kids need is to see Mom and Dad work through the conflict in a healthy way. Then kids have a sense of how to deal with conflict in their own marriages when, not if, conflict occurs.

Later I asked Dad about this fight. He seemed a bit embarrassed about it. I guess we all would feel the same. Yet he gave me another great insight, which I would be remiss not to share with you.

"David," he said, "conflict is a great opportunity in marriage."

It was my time to squint my eyes in disbelief. Conflict is an opportunity? I run from conflict like an Olympic sprinter!

"But it is!" he said. "Conflict shows areas of the marriage that need work. I was too busy. Mom was right. I was overwhelmed, and Mom wasn't empathizing with my life situation at that moment. I was right, too. Therefore, after our emotions settled down, and we began to talk civilly with one another, we both began to make decisions to address the real issues.

"What we both discovered is conflict is a pathway to more intimacy. If used rightly, it can be a wonderful gift from God."

I went from the fear and anxiety of hearing "I must leave" to the comfort of "Conflict is a gift from God."

It continues to be a necessary life lesson. I hope my kids have learned it. They've seen the conflict. They've also seen the hugs after the conflict.

I hope they now have a few hints on how to handle conflict in marriage.

The fact is, "The closer two people become, the more they bump."

But there's another life lesson about marriage Dad taught me.

Conflict is a gift from God.

I hope you can learn it, too, for your own marriages, but especially for your children.

And your children's children.

Part Two

Parenting

*"I can always buy a new car,
but I can't buy a new you."*

M y brother Howard is five years older than I am. Our personalities are different. I was passive and naturally compliant to my parents' wishes; Howard would stretch the limits and see how far he could go.

One such episode with Howard is forever etched in my mind.

We had just purchased a new car. It was the family's prize. One night, Howard wanted to go out with some friends. He asked Dad if he could borrow the new car. Dad reluctantly agreed.

Later that night the phone rang. It was one of those calls every parent dreads. Howard had been in an accident. The car was totaled. It seemed Howard was all right.

Dad piled us all in the other family car. We drove to the home of one of our church members where Dad had been told Howard would be. There was a deafening silence in the car as we approached. I was around eleven years old at the time. I was curious to see how Dad would handle this crisis. I was also a bit excited to see Howard receive some good old-fashioned punishment. I guess you can call it sibling rivalry.

Dad approached the front door with a stern face. I knew Howard was going to get it! Dad knocked. Our friends politely opened the door. Dad, Mom, and the rest of us entered the room. Howard was in the corner, crying.

Dad moved toward Howard. Howard took a few steps back. Dad grabbed Howard by the shoulders, then drew him close. For several minutes they hugged . . . and cried.

"Drat," I thought, "is that all that is going to happen? Howard deserves more than that!"

"Dad," Howard finally said, "I wrecked your new car. I completely wrecked it."

Then Dad spoke words that forever echo in my mind. "Son," he said, "I can always buy a new car, but I cannot buy a new you. I'm so glad you're OK."

As he should have been, Dad was more concerned with his son than a car, more concerned about a person than a possession.

However, here's a part of the story I never knew until a conversation with Dad a few months ago. We were reminiscing about this story. I shared with Dad that I admired how well he handled it. I told him it had had a profound impact on me.

"Well," he responded, "you don't know the half of it. When your mother and I were dating, one night I asked your grandfather [whom I never knew; he died when Mom was around twenty] to borrow his treasured car. It was his pride and joy. We were double-dating with another couple who were dear friends.

"I was driving a bit too fast. I approached a turn and didn't sufficiently slow down. I lost control of the car, and it spun off the road. It turned over on its side and spun around a few times. Fortunately, no one was hurt. However, you can well imagine my fear and trepidation as I approached your mother's home, knowing your grandfather would know of the accident and the demolition of his prized car.

"I entered the home. Your mother's father approached me. I began to shrink back. He grabbed my shoulders and pulled me toward him. We embraced. I cried. Then he pulled me away and said some words I'll never forget: 'Howard,' he said, 'I can always buy another car, but I can't buy a new you or another daughter.'"

I suddenly got it. Dad was simply treating Howard the way he had been treated in a similar situation. In essence, my grandfather was parenting my brother! Dad knew the power of my grandfather's words to him. Therefore, he knew what Howard needed.

My daughter just started driving. My two sons are several years away from this experience. I pray none of them will ever wreck either of our cars—especially the new one! However, if they should, I know how to respond. I can only hope and pray my knowledge will be translated into the correct action.

Cars can be replaced. Children cannot.

My grandfather taught my dad this truth. My dad gave it to his sons. I want to give it to my children.

Isn't it amazing to think about? If we are parenting rightly now, we are parenting the faith, values, and principles of children in the twenty-second century!

That's a parenting principle worth pondering.

*"You've never lied to me before,
and I believe you now."*

M rs. Sanders was our neighbor. She was a nice, elderly lady who sometimes became involved in another neighbor's business when she didn't need to be involved.

One of those times she became involved with me.

I was playing with some kids who lived on the other side of Mrs. Sanders. We were playing basketball, cops-and-robbers, and anything else that would help pass the time during the summer.

When I arrived home that evening, my parents had stern looks on their faces. Dad finally began the conversation.

"Son," he said, "Mrs. Sanders just called."

I had a bad feeling it wasn't going to get much better with his next words. I meekly responded, "Yes, sir?"

"She said she heard you kids playing next door. She said you all were quite rowdy."

I thought to myself, "Well, so far so good. We were rowdy, but so what?"

Dad continued, "She said that she heard you cursing like a sailor. She said that the words that came from your mouth would embarrass any parent, but especially us, being in the ministry."

I was dumbfounded. I wasn't a perfect kid growing up, but for some reason I always refused to curse. I carefully guarded every word that came from my mouth. Maybe it was because I didn't like the taste of soap!

I therefore vehemently denied the charges. I even cried. "I didn't do it, Dad, honest, I didn't say one curse word." It probably was my friend Steve. He didn't hesitate to let a few bad words fly from his mouth. But I wasn't about to tell on him.

"You're telling me the absolute truth?" Dad asked me.

Through my tears, I nodded yes.

Then, without hesitation, he said, "Well, then I believe you. You've never lied to me about anything, and I believe you now."

He and Mom then marched next door and told Mrs. Sanders what I had said. They told her they believed me—it must have been another kid swearing, and that was that.

Mrs. Sanders didn't like their response one bit. I don't think she spoke to us for another six months.

It didn't matter to me. My parents had believed me. They trusted me. I didn't do it. I knew it. My parents honored my word.

To this day, that experience stands out in my mind. To the best of my knowledge, I have never lied to either of my parents.

Moreover, the experience entrenched within me a deep desire always to tell the truth. Their confidence in me motivated a greater desire to be honest.

Kids are human, too. When treated with respect, they want to be respectful.

Mrs. Sanders helped me realize this truth. Although it was painful at the time, it's a lesson I'm presently teaching my kids.

In a strange way, a belated thanks, Mrs. Sanders, is owed to you.

Thanks!

*"Don't worry what people are thinking about you.
They're not thinking about you at all. They are
too busy thinking about themselves."*

I considered transferring from the University of North Carolina after my sophomore year. I hadn't played much. Two prep school All-Americans had just been recruited at my position. However, after an arduous soul search, I finally decided you can't solve a problem by running away from it. I decided to honor my commitment, even if it meant never playing basketball at UNC.

After I had made the decision to return to UNC for my final two seasons, it was a huge relief. Except for one matter: I was terribly worried about what people might think.

As I had been contemplating the decision, I had told some people. Obviously the athletic department knew about the decision. I worried that the word had spread far and wide. I worried about what people would think.

I had made my decision to remain at UNC. I was going to pursue my dream to play at UNC. The next night I shared with Dad my one concern about what people would think.

Regarding this subject, he didn't hesitate. He knew I had a people-pleasing side. I suspect he does, too. In fact, I suspect everyone does, to some degree or another. But I think Dad has a particular dislike for this monster. Perhaps he, too, had to slay it a time or two in his life.

He looked me straight in the eye and said, "Son, don't you worry about what other people think about you. Take my word for it. They're not thinking about you at all. They're too busy thinking about themselves."

If there is any one piece of counsel I remember from his experience in ministry, it's this one: People will suck you dry. They will take as much of you as they can, oftentimes without a "thank you." If you constantly worry about what they think about this or that, you'll forever be in a frenzied state.

Besides, if they know they can't control you with their opinions of you, they will quickly move on to another person they can control.

To my dad and my friend, I just want to say, "Thank you."

It's a thought that has revolutionized my life and ministry.

Now, how do I teach this one to my kids?

"Kids spell love T-I-M-E."

■

Dad grew up during the Depression. His mother died when he was twelve, and his family never had much. Dad vividly remembers his own dad going from job to job. He especially remembers the long jobless periods.

They had to move in with family. Dad describes the two small rooms and the large numbers sharing space and food. The times were indeed difficult.

Dad was a fairly good athlete. He enjoyed sports. However, because of the tough economic times and his own family's situation, he was unable to participate in any extracurricular activities. When school was out, he had to come home and complete chores. When they were completed, it was time for bed. The next day was more of the same.

One can understand why Dad became a very hard worker. His admirable work ethic was forged in this environment. He graduated from high school when he was fifteen. He achieved at every academic level and was graduated from Moravian College in Bethlehem, Pennsylvania, with honors. Thereafter he experienced and accepted God's call into the ministry. He attended Duke University Divinity School where he studied philosophy. Kant, Schopenaur, and Tillich were familiar names to him. Again, he was an honors student. From there he received his master of divinity degree.

Frankly, Dad wanted to succeed. He was partly driven by a positive God-given work ethic. Mostly, however, he was driven to avoid, for himself or for his family to come, the deep, dark, hungry days of the Depression.

Dad was a successful pastor. After my brother Howard was born, Dad continued to pour himself into the ministry, building successful, growing churches wherever he went. He was upward and mobile. Everyone admired his hard work and success.

However, in the process of becoming very successful, he forgot my brother Howard. Dad failed to see the signs of need in Howard's life for a daddy. Night after night he was away, attending meetings, visiting the sick and needy, preparing a message. For example, Dad shared with me once that, from September to Christmas one year, he didn't spend one night at home. Looking back, he's not proud of that reality. However, it was the Depression work ethic drummed into his psyche.

Howard's willingness to stretch limits only exacerbated the problem. Before Dad knew it, Howard was a teenager and not exactly reflecting the life to which Dad had committed himself. Their relationship was strained.

I've loved sports since I can remember. When I was given an army of toy soldiers, I immediately renamed every one and transformed them into sports players. On the floor of our den, I played football, basketball, and baseball games according to the season. I would become absorbed in this activity for hours. Moreover, I played on every sports team I could. I must have inherited the athletic genes Dad was never able to develop.

One evening, when I was around ten or so, Dad came home from work a bit early. Right before dinner, he looked at me and asked, "You want to go to a Charlotte Hornets baseball game tonight?" (Charlotte, in the 1960s, possessed a minor league baseball team named the Hornets. That's where the present NBA franchise got the name.)

I couldn't believe my ears. Would I like to go? I wanted to go anywhere sports were being played! I yelled, "I'd love to go, Dad."

So we went to the game and sat on the right field side, about ten rows back. I can still remember being on the tiptoe of expectation, jumping for a glimpse of the field as we entered the stadium. I can still hear the crack of the bat, the smell of freshly cut grass, the announced names of the players on our team (and the names of a few on the other team!). We bought a snow cone at the bottom of the fifth inning, halfway through the game. It was a blowout. The Hornets were winning by a huge score. At the end of the seventh, Dad asked if I wanted to go home since the game was already decided.

"Of course not!" I said. I wanted to see the entire game. I wanted to drink up every single second of being with my dad. Who cared about sleep? Homework could wait! I was with my dad!

We arrived home well after ten o'clock. I wasn't even tired the next day at school. It was an evening I'll never forget.

Guess what ? There were other evenings just the same. On a regular basis thereafter, Dad would come home, and we'd repeat the just mentioned story. We'd sit in the same place. We'd always buy a snow cone at the end of the fifth inning. Orange was my favorite.

One time the St. Louis Cardinals played an exhibition game against the Hornets. Dad again took me. He knew one of their pitchers, Vinegar Bend Mizell. Dad had married Mizell and his wife. After the game, Dad took me to the door of the locker room and offered to take me inside to meet his pitcher friend and some of the other players like Stan Musial. I was painfully shy and emphatically told him that I didn't want to do that. I regret it to this day.

Later, as I began to develop some basketball prowess, I noticed Dad always took me to the games. In high school, he came to practically every game. I think he may have missed one or two. In college, he came to my games at the University of North Carolina as often as possible. Every season, Mom and he would plan a trip to catch several games. They were always at the Atlantic Coast Conference tournament games.

My senior season, when we were playing in the post-season National Invitational Tournament, Dad and Mom flew to New York to see the games . . . except the last one. He had a wedding he felt obliged to perform. He flew back to Orlando, Florida, and watched the game on television until the wedding began. Afterward he ran back into his office to catch the remaining moments. He even had a television executive at a local station record the game so he could later watch it in its entirety. He also wanted me to see it when I was home on spring break.

Then I went to Europe and played in the European professional leagues for three years. You guessed correctly. Every year, he and Mom took a trip to visit with me and see me play.

To say that he was involved with me is an understatement. He was always there when I needed him.

But he wasn't there for Howard. As a result, Howard wandered for several years. Finally, by God's grace, Howard found his life's calling in the ministry, and he and Dad are fine. Howard understands what drove Dad, and Dad, well, Dad told me something I'll always remember about our lives together and some of the mistakes he made with Howard.

I had asked him why he invited me to the Hornet's baseball game when I was around ten. He sighed. Then he said, "I knew I'd lost one son because of my driven, workaholic habits. I wasn't going to lose the other son. Kids spell love T-I-M-E."

I'm doing the same with my kids. I'm at every game, even coaching some of their teams. I don't want to lose them either.

I've learned this truth: Kids spell love T-I-M-E.

I've heard Dad say this. I've seen him live it.

It's a lesson well worth learning.

But mostly it's a lesson well worth living.

"Howard needs me."

■

The last chapter, I hope, clued you in to the reality that my older brother Howard had a rebellious streak while growing up. It manifested itself during the teenage years. It became fully realized in his early adult years.

Howard is extremely gifted as a musician. He sings extraordinarily well, and earned a voice scholarship to Westminster College in Futon, Missouri. Amazingly, his voice sounds like Dad's, who is equally gifted as a singer and musician.

After graduation from college, Howard moved to Nashville, Tennessee, with his new wife. He enrolled at Vanderbilt Theological Seminary, but he was much more concerned with developing and advancing his musical career. While in Nashville, he signed a recording contract with a local recording company. He wrote songs and sang in nightclubs. The Promised Land of pop glory was always one elusive step away, he was told.

Slowly but surely, his life degraded. His wife left him. He moved into an apartment with a local waitress from one of the clubs in which he sang. They had two children together and, to the best of my knowledge, lived a common-law marriage over a period of years.

I remember visiting him one time in Nashville right after I had graduated from college. He told me wild stories of spiritual forces in his apartment, wigs flying across the room unaided, being in touch with the invisible world. I felt strange in his presence and tried to confront him about his lifestyle. It did no good.

The hits never came. He and his now-common-law wife then moved to Los Angeles. A new record company expressed interest. He was sure they would lead him to musical glory. While living there, he continued to sing in nightclubs. His lifestyle was late to bed and late to rise. He became involved with a man who was convinced he was Jesus Christ reincarnated. He gathered around him twelve people who supposedly were the twelve disciples. Howard was Thaddeus Jude.

During my first year in seminary in Atlanta, Georgia, I flew to Los Angeles to interview for a potential job and also to visit with Howard. It was Nashville revisited, only worse. The dark feel in his apartment made my hair stand on edge. Howard's friends seemed typecast for a horror flick! I couldn't wait to leave.

Howard's life in Los Angeles only spiraled downward. He was doing drugs. He was involved in the occult. It was sad and apparently hopeless.

The next thing I knew Howard was back in Nashville with another recording opportunity. Again, prosperity and success were right around the corner. He continued to write songs; however, his common-law wife was not with him. They had separated in California.

However, Howard's bad habits continued. So did his depression. No one knew how deep it would become.

We were all home one evening in Orlando, Florida, when the phone rang. It was one of Howard's friends. When Dad got on the phone, all he heard was, "Your son needs you." Evidently Howard had tried to take his own life.

I remember Dad immediately packing his bags. Frankly, I also remember my own pride coming to the surface, smugly thinking to myself, "Why are you doing this, Dad? He made his bed. Let him lie in it." Today, with a much more balanced spiritual equilibrium, I wonder which God hated more: Howard's flirtations with the occult and personal irresponsibility or my self-righteousness!

I also remember turning to Dad while he was packing and asking, "Where are you going?"

He answered, "I'm flying to Nashville. Howard is in trouble."

Arrogantly I responded, "Why are you going to do that?"

Without blinking, he said, "David, Howard needs me."

With that, he closed his suitcase and went to the airport.

Howard couldn't believe it when he opened his eyes and Dad was there. It was the beginning of healing for him. They talked and talked. Lost ground was made up. God gave Howard His healing love through Dad that day. I don't know the exact conversation, but I'd guess much forgiveness was expressed between them.

Several years later, Howard was ordained into the ministry. Today, he leads a successful, alive, and growing church in Daytona Beach, Florida. He has married a beautiful, vivacious woman named Ramona. In every way possible his life has been restored and redeemed.

I believe Howard's success is largely linked to Dad's willingness to go to Howard in his deepest, darkest hour. Dad's presence in this time of need spoke more loudly and powerfully than all the previous words spoken between them.

I believe it's also attributable to Dad's (and Mom's) relentless prayers offered on Howard's behalf. They always believed he would come back to the foundation laid in his early years. They always believed God's hands were still on him, even in his early thirties when everything seemed hopeless, when prayers had been persistently offered for many years. Dad believed the acorn would not fall far from the tree. He believed God would intercede, some way, somehow.

Dad prayed incessantly. And he went when called. He talked a lot about God's love for us. He embodied God's love to us.

"Howard needs me."

Our kids need us . . . especially in the hardest times.

Frankly, though, they need their parents all the time.

That's because love is spelled T-I-M-E.

*"You're always a parent,
no matter what age they are."*

■

My sister Carolyn is three years older than I am, two years younger than Howard. She's a great gal, though she, too, has been through some tough times in her life.

I'm sure it wasn't easy for her to be sandwiched between Howard and me. As mentioned previously, Howard has an exceptional musical ability. He sang in church, school, and community plays. Both Carolyn and I were constantly asked while growing up, "Do you sing, too." Frankly, it became quite tiresome.

Then I discovered basketball. As I matured and grew to be almost six feet eight inches tall, I was recruited by schools all over the country. Carolyn was sandwiched between two successful brothers. I'm sure it was frustrating for her as she sought an identity of her own.

She married right out of college and had a child. The marriage didn't work. Interestingly, I remember when her divorce occurred, and knowledge of Howard's common-law marriage was fairly well known, Mom, out of the blue one evening, said to me and Dad, "If anyone asks us about our children's marriage situations, we will tell them the truth and hold our heads high."

But I know it hurt them both. They loved their kids, but ached, as they knew their kids were aching.

Carolyn continued to date through the years, but could never find the right man. As she moved into her fifties, Dad became increasingly worried about her. He wanted her happiness beyond all else, but he also worried what would happen to her if she ever became ill. Who would take care of her? How could she take care of herself financially? Dad was experiencing what a friend recently said to me about parenting: "You're only as happy as your unhappiest child."

One evening, while talking about Carolyn, Dad heaved a sigh and said to me, "Well, Son, even though she's in her fifties and I'm in my eighties, I still worry about her. I think I could die happily right now if I knew she was happy and would be taken care of."

A little while back, Carolyn called and said she had met a man. His name is Dan. They were in the same church. She, too, is on the tall side, approaching five feet eleven inches, and Dan was shorter than she. But she said they felt comfortable together. She said she liked him.

Friendship eventually grew into love. Carolyn recently told me she has redefined her understanding of what love is. It's care and common concern. It's mutual enjoyment. It's spiritual camaraderie. As she wrote in her most recent Christmas card, "We met. We became best friends. We fell in love. I married my best friend."

Dad and my brother Howard recently married them at Howard's church. They're very happy together. Dan's a great guy. They're forming the kind of unconditional love Mom and Dad have for one another. For the first time in decades, I see a smile on Carolyn's face.

Not long ago, after the wedding, Dad said to me, "Well, I guess now I can die a happy man."

Then he said something else I'll never forget, "I guess, too, you're always a parent, no matter what age they are."

Every parent reading this knows it's true.

"If a man doesn't have his word, he has nothing."

■

The three of us children were like most children; we wanted what other people had. We also wanted the products advertised on television. We didn't want to be strange or ostracized. Materialism began to engulf this minister's home, though his salary didn't come close to satisfying our greed.

We knew Dad ultimately controlled the purse strings, especially on the big stuff such as radios, bicycles, and new beds. When we really wanted something, he was our target.

We also knew that if we could get him to say the magic words, "I promise," what we wanted would be ours. Therefore, whenever we would ask for something, and he would show the slightest inclination to buy it for us, we would ask, "Promise Dad? Say, 'I promise.'"

He never would. He would never say, "I promise," when it came to buying things.

Why? Because his word was his bond. He was such a man of integrity that if he ever uttered the words "I promise," he felt himself bound to do what he said. Integrity for Dad meant doing what you said. It meant your outside life matched your inside life. The two were integrated.

That's why, when badgered by us kids to buy something, he would never say, "I promise." Instead, he would always say, "I'm not promising. We'll see." Then he'd try with every ounce of his being to buy us what we desired.

Later I asked him why he was so particular about never uttering these words to us children. I'll never forget his answer.

He simply said, "If a man doesn't have his word, he has nothing."

He then continued, "Do you know, David, that when I was brought up, during the Depression, people could not afford lawyers and the expense of legal contracts when they were making a deal. Oftentimes, people in different professions exchanged goods. Each needed the other's goods simply to live. Therefore, when we exchanged these goods, all we could do was shake hands and believe the other would deliver simply by his spoken word.

"You know," he continued, "it worked pretty well. If someone didn't deliver, his word became no good. And the minute he lost his good word, the moment people doubted whether he would deliver, they stopped doing business with him. We really needed one another simply to live. It's funny how hunger can be a very positive motivator for honesty!"

Sadly, there is still hunger in the world today, but for most of us, it isn't one of the motivators for honesty. However, what should still motivate us is that our word is all we have. It shows the integrity of our heart.

It's simply the right thing to do.

In the past, today, and always!

"Are you OK? Please come here."

When we three kids were growing up, Friday night was family night. We'd pop popcorn and sit in front of the television. All of us looked forward to this time, except when Howard and Carolyn became teenagers!

Being the youngest, I couldn't always stay awake on Friday nights. Often I'd fall asleep on Mom or Dad's shoulder. I can still vividly remember the ritual whenever this would happen. Dad would pick me up and put my head on his shoulder. He would carry me up the stairs and put me to bed.

To this day, I remember the smell of his cologne on his cheeks. (I think it was Old Spice.) It would be my last memory before I'd fall asleep in my bed—Dad tucking me in and kissing me good night and the smell of his cologne.

In my twenties, I did graduate studies in counseling at the University of Florida. It was after European basketball and before my calling to enter ministry. I was uncertain what I wanted to do with my life. Therefore, my dear friend John Lotz, then the head coach at the University of Florida, offered me a graduate assistantship to work with the basketball program while pursuing graduate studies.

Dad was the pastor of First Presbyterian Church in Orlando, Florida at the time. I would regularly go home to see my parents during weekends.

One weekend Mom and Dad wanted to take a trip to Winston-Salem, North Carolina, to assist in the wedding of a niece, my first cousin. They asked me if I would housesit while they were away. I enthusiastically agreed. I would be able to come home and rest from a very busy, tiring schedule in graduate school.

It was a Friday night. I'd fallen asleep in their bed downstairs (my bedroom was upstairs). At about four in the morning, I heard noises in the house. I thought it was just the foundation shifting or something like that. I went back to sleep. Suddenly, the lights in their bedroom went on and off very quickly. I jolted to my elbows. Another flicker of light allowed me to see a gun about six inches from my head. I heard a voice that gruffly said, "Roll over, put the pillows over your head, or you're a dead man."

I quickly did what I was asked to do!

I could tell the light in the room went on. They then proceeded to cut telephone wire to tie my hands behind my back and my feet together. For the next forty-five minutes they ransacked the house. I suspect they were looking for drugs. Several times they asked me if my dad was a doctor. They must have seen his prescriptions with his title, Dr. Chadwick. I tried to tell them he was a minister, but evidently they didn't believe me.

While they ransacked the house, one of them sat on the bed and constantly poked my ribs and my temple, saying inane things like, "You're a dead man. How does it feel to be ready to die?" I really did think I was going to die. It's amazing how quickly one develops a theology of the afterlife with a gun to his head!

Suddenly, the room became quiet. They had left. I sat up. Somehow I was able to free my feet but not my hands from the telephone wire. I ran to the phone in the kitchen and knocked it off with my chin. It fell to the floor. I then dialed the operator with my forefinger behind my back. I told her to please call the police. I'd just been robbed.

I was also able to dial my sister's number. She, too, lived in Orlando with her then-husband. They and the police arrived about the same time. I was untied and quizzed. It wasn't much fun.

Carolyn immediately called Mom and Dad in Winston-Salem to tell them what had happened. I don't know exactly what was said. I do know they immediately drove back to Orlando from North Carolina. Dad later told me there was little conversation between him and Mom during the almost twelve-hour drive. Their son and home had been violated. They were in shock. By the evening, they were home.

What I remember most clearly from this incident is not the stark, rude awakening in the middle of the night. Nor is my sharpest memory the gun in my side and head. Indeed, what I remember most is when Dad walked into the room after his return from the trip.

He looked at me for a few moments. Then, with a quivering voice, he asked, "Are you OK?" When I nodded affirmatively, he said, "Please come here."

We walked toward one another and embraced. Although now four inches taller than he, it was my head that once again nestled on his shoulder, the same position I assumed as a child when he would carry me to bed on family nights.

As we embraced, we both sobbed. I was OK. Therefore, he was OK.

But then it happened. That smell . . . that unmistakable smell. It was his cologne. He hadn't changed it in twenty years. It was his favorite when I was a child. It was his favorite now.

I smelled his love. I was feeling his love. It was an unforgettable moment.

Parents, I recognize we live in a world where much inappropriate touching exists. I understand many adults have wrongly used touching with children. Many adults today are still feeling the pain from this kind of physical abuse.

However, for those of us who genuinely love our children and want the best for them, let's not forget that physical touching and the smells that often accompany this closeness should be gifts to our children. They help define and express our love. They are smells and touches that create memories of love for a lifetime.

Plus, they're needed whether you're five or twenty-five, especially in times of need.

Corrie ten Boon, the noted Christian author and survivor of a Nazi war camp in World War II, once said that one of the ways she was able to survive was the memory of her father when she was a child. Every night he would enter her room and stroke her forehead. He would lean over and tell her how much he loved her. She would smell his hair lotion.

In bed at night in those horrid conditions, she would feel the heavenly Father's love, stroking her forehead. Plus, she would remember those smells that symbolized her earthly father's care.

And she would go to sleep, trusting her Father in heaven would take care of her.

Please don't ever discount the importance of love expressed through physical touching and the unique human smells that accompany it.

It helps get us through life.

Trust me.

I know from first-hand experience.

*"It's because I love you that
I am going to discipline you."*

◼

We were vacationing in South Florida. I was approaching my teenage years, learning to stretch my wings. Howard was away somewhere. Carolyn was with us on the trip. We really do like each other, but that week it seemed questionable.

It was one of those steamy nights in South Florida. She did something to irritate me. I didn't like it one bit. Finally, I yelled at her to stop it. (Why does this remind me of present scenarios with my almost-teenage son and his sister who is three years older?)

I heard that distinctive baritone voice from the other room.

"David," he boomed, "stop that yelling. If you do that one more time I am going to come in there and discipline you. I will not tolerate yelling."

I calmed down. Carolyn did too. I told her to leave me alone. I didn't want to talk to her or be with her any longer.

She did it again. I yelled again.

Dad's shadow was in the frame of the door within seconds.

"Son," he said, "I must discipline you. I warned you. Now I must act."

I was petrified. I had experienced Dad's firm hand of discipline before. I wanted no part of it now. I quickly thought of a plan.

"Dad," I asked, "don't you love me?"

It was a brilliant plan. Dad would contemplate his love for his youngest child. He would think about our newfound times together, the snow cones at the Hornet's baseball games, . . . the terror on my face!

I continued, "If you really love me, Dad, you won't punish me!"

Without missing a beat, he responded, "It's because I love you I'm going to punish you."

He punished me.

But I've come to believe that it was truly love that motivated him to discipline. It cost him something, too. It cost him energy. It cost him emotion. I'm also certain it cost him sleep! I know this truth because I've become a parent!

I've also learned through this that sometimes God disciplines his children, too. It's not because he hates us. It's not because he desires to torment us. Like Dad, he sees behavior that is hurting us. He knows if left untended, this behavior could seriously damage us in the future.

Thanks, Dad, for loving enough to discipline!

"I trust you. I don't trust your hormones."

◼

I guess in some ways Dad was a bit old-fashioned by today's standards. However, he had some rules he wanted us to follow, especially in the area of dating.

One night I secured a date. That in itself should show us all God still works miracles. My sophomore year I was six feet five inches tall and weighed a whopping one hundred and fifty pounds. Yes, I heard every skinny joke imaginable. "I bet you sunburn on one side and peel on the other." "I bet you have to put in the plug when you take a shower so you don't go down the drain with the water." "I bet if you turned sideways and stuck out your tongue, you'd look like a zipper!" Ha, ha . . . funny, funny.

Anyway, I did actually secure a date. She was a cute girl, and I was proud of myself for getting up the nerve to ask her out and then having her say, "Yes"! She was all of five feet one inches tall. I can still vividly remember walking into the movie theater and looking at us together in a mirror. I couldn't see her! And I could see myself from the belt buckle up.

Naively, I told Dad what I was planning on doing. For some part of the evening I was going to be alone with this girl in the car. He told me I couldn't do that; I needed to be with a group of people.

I loudly objected. I told him this was a good girl. He was being unreasonable.

Then I asked, "Don't you trust me, Dad?"

I shouldn't have asked. He had the answer.

"Oh, I trust you, Son. I just don't trust your hormones!"

I have a teenage daughter right now. My son is rapidly approaching puberty. I guess my youngest will also one day be a teenager, as much as I'd like to freeze time and keep him young.

Guess what? I really trust them. They're great kids.

But I don't trust their hormones.

I'm certain I'll insist on group dating. I'm sure I will particularly hate the idea of any of them alone with a date in a car.

Thanks a lot, Dad!

I only hope your grandkids will one day similarly thank you!

Or blame you.

It wasn't my idea!

But I've come to like it.

*"It was just a dress rehearsal
before the main performance."*

R emember your first love? Remember the feelings? Like
the Beatles said, "Well, my heart went boom when I
crossed that room. . . ."

My first real deep-seated affection occurred during my two
years at the University of Florida. One moment we were just
two strangers in a crowded room; the next, our emotions
skyrocketed. My hormones, which my Dad didn't trust, were
out of control.

We dated for a few months. Everything seemed perfect. I
drove to her home in South Florida. We were going to spend a
weekend together. She came by to pick me up at my hotel room.

We spent an absolutely delightful evening together—dinner, walking, and talking. It was late. She drove me back to
the room.

She was about to say good night. She paused for a moment, awkwardly stammering a bit. Finally, she blurted out,

"You know, David, it's been fun being with you, but I think we should stop seeing one another."

I was stunned. I couldn't believe it. Out of the blue, she was telling me this whirlwind relationship was over? I asked why. I wanted an explanation. I was dumbfounded.

But she offered no reasons. After another five minutes of my awkward questions, she closed the door and walked out of my life . . . forever. Oh, I tried to write and call. I received no response. As the days became weeks, I slowly accepted the fact that it was over. However, the hurt persisted. I needed a reason, but none was given. None *would* be given.

So I wondered and questioned. Did I have bad breath? Was I too tall? Was it because my eyes were hazel? Any reason would have been better than no reason. The rejection was bad enough. The rejection without explanation was devastating to my self-esteem. My soul was shattered.

That lonely, startling night, I did the only thing I knew to do; I called Mom and Dad. It helped a tiny bit to hear their voices. When I told them what had happened, Dad calmly said, "Why don't you drive home tomorrow?" I did.

The long drive from South Florida to Orlando seemed to drag on endlessly. Mom and Dad were waiting for me. We talked awhile. I cried a bit. Dad and I were left alone when Mom had to run an errand. Neither of us spoke for a while.

Finally, he uttered words that began the healing process for me. It didn't happen immediately, but as I pondered these words, they began to make sense.

He simply said, "Sometimes, Son, you need a dress rehearsal before the main performance."

About two years later I met Marilynn. Now, over twenty years later, I understand how profound Dad's words were. The pain I experienced forced me to consider what kind of girl I needed to marry. I began an examination of my strengths and weaknesses. I saw more and more how my previous friend and I were not right for one another. Frankly, we both were spared.

Moreover, at that time of my life, I had not yet responded to God's call to ministry. Had I married her, I have no assurance she would have shared that call to ministry. Indeed, sadly, I have every reason to believe we would have ended up in divorce court!

Marilynn has been my perfect mate. She's the true love of my life. The other attraction was mostly emotional and hormonal; I was a twenty-something guy wanting emotional closeness, not a lifelong partner.

So if you have been ditched recently, don't despair. There is a time and place for everything.

The ball game is not over. There is another at-bat for you.

And remember, in the immortal words of baseball player and philosopher Yogi Berra, "It ain't over till it's over."

My sister Carolyn met and married Dan in her fifties after a failed marriage. Marilynn, the love of my life, came to me after a painful rejection.

God knows your pain. Trust him. Keep believing. He has a plan.

Most likely, your past relationship was just a dress rehearsal before the main performance.

"I'm proud of you, Son."

■

My brief encounter with the girl from South Florida was indeed devastating. My feelings were injured for several months thereafter. One of my good friends kept saying to me a line from a song by Jim Croce: "A good time man like [you] ain't got no business singing the blues." But my heart ached. Life didn't hold much purpose for me.

I didn't know it at the time, but what I was really searching for was purpose in my life. You see, while growing up, many people used to tease me, saying, "You're going to grow up just like your dad." I didn't want to grow up like Dad. I didn't want anything to do with ministry. I saw him come home fatigued from dealing with ornery church members. I sometimes didn't see him come home at all. He was responding to crises or preparing another message. No, ministry was Dad's call. I wanted nothing to do with it.

At that point in my life, I was wrestling with two directions. I was earning a degree in counseling. I had practically completed the necessary work for a doctorate. But I still loved basketball. I was wondering about coaching. Or perhaps a combination of counseling and coaching was a possibility.

But when my life was turned around by the infamous rejection in South Florida, I didn't know where I would turn.

I didn't need to turn anywhere. My purpose would come to me.

In a lonely apartment in Gainesville, Florida, in 1976, I reached the end of my rope. I was sick and tired of being sick and tired. Finally, in desperation, I cried out to God.

"OK," I said, "I give up. I hurt. I'm tired. If you want me in ministry, I'll go."

The room was silent. What happened next is difficult to explain. I heard a voice. Inward or outward, I'm not sure. I am sure I heard it.

It simply said, "David. I love you. Before the foundations of the world were ever created, I chose you to proclaim my love to this world."

I shook my head. I thought, "Say what? Would you mind please repeating what you just said?"

There was silence. No more voices spoke. But I was sure what I had heard.

For several hours I contemplated what had happened. But I knew. I knew what I was supposed to do. I knew I was called into ministry. I needed to enter seminary. It needed to occur immediately.

I called home. Mom answered. I told her to get Dad on the telephone line. Then I told them what had happened.

There was silence. I think there were then some tears. I am certain what Dad said next.

"I'm proud of you, Son. I'm very, very proud of you, Son."

And I was proud to be his son.

I don't know if your children are grown. It doesn't matter. No matter what their ages, tell them you're proud of them. Somehow, we need it. It's medicine to a battered soul.

You may even want to say it daily. It's that meaningful.

Trust me. I know.

"You are who you are, not what you do."

One of the sicknesses of our performance-based culture is people constantly trying to succeed, driving themselves to accomplish endless goals. As a result, people have come to believe that how they perform equals who they are. No message could be more deadly and dangerous to a workaholic, stressed-out society like ours.

That's not to say there isn't value in performing and succeeding at a task. When my son Michael was barely six years old, I had a sense that he was ready to ride a two-wheeler bike without the training wheels. We went out to our carport, I balanced the bike from the rear, and he began pedaling. I let go and he took off! He rode that bike for the rest of the afternoon and for days to come.

At the end of the day, while putting him to bed, he turned to his mom and said, "Mom, today was the best day of my life."

It does feel good to succeed. But we need to balance this with the fact that our success doesn't define who we are or how much we're loved.

That's one of the reasons I love Dad so much. I never felt his love for me was performance-based. If ever he sensed that I was defining my worth based on my performance, whether in academics or sports, he would always say, "You are who you are, not what you do."

That's not to say Dad would never correct a mistake or encourage harder work. He would. And when he did, I would be encouraged to work harder to succeed. He, too, knew it feels good to succeed. However, he never defined his love for me by performance. His love was always a free gift.

All Dad ever asked of me, all he ever wanted from me, in every area of my life, was my best effort. He knew the rest would fall in line if I just desired to do and be my best.

It's all I want from my kids.

It's all God wants from us.

After all, he did name us human beings, not human doings.

"Did you do your best?"

■

In parenting, one of our more anxious moments is when our children bring home their report cards. We glance nervously at the column where the grades are listed. If we see mostly As or Bs, we release our breath and politely thank God.

However, if Cs are seen, our hearts start racing. If there's a D, or that dreaded other letter, it's time to dial 911 and ask for the medics!

Perhaps there's an even better response than overwhelming exhilaration or cardiac arrest when examining our kids' performance in any area. I think there is, and once again Dad has shown me the way.

Whenever we kids would bring home a report card, Dad would, like all good parents, study the grade column. You could never read his face regarding what he was thinking. He would carefully examine the A . . . or the B . . . or the C (obviously, the Ds or Fs never occurred with me or my brother or sister!). Yet from Dad's perspective, the grade didn't immediately concern him the most. The first question out of his mouth after he perused the report card was always the same.

He'd look at us and simply ask, "Did you do your best?" If we answered, "Yes," he would thank us for a job well done, working so hard, and doing our best. Then he would return to what he was doing. If, however, we said, "No," he'd begin a dialogue with us regarding why we hadn't done our best. He'd try to find out the forces impeding us from our best effort and eliminate them forever. Distractions, laziness, emotional pain—whatever it was, he'd try to eradicate it from our lives so we could do our best.

That's all he ever asked. He believed the best results would surely be accomplished with our best efforts. The results indeed became secondary to the efforts.

As I am presently raising my own three children, I'm appreciating Dad's wisdom in this area more and more. Kids want to know if they're loved unconditionally, a love not based on performance. If the love is performance-based, the child never knows if they've done enough to please the parent. These are the questions they're asking as they hand the report cards to their parents: "Is a B good enough?" "What if I'm incapable of making an A?" "Will I still be loved?" . . . At least that was the case with me!

When my kids hand me their report cards, I'm doing the same thing my Dad did. All I want from them is their best effort. All I desire is for them to look me in the eye and say, "Dad, I did my best." Then they receive excited hugs, whether the grade is an A or a D.

After all, that's the way God has loved us. We didn't have to perform perfectly before he chose to love us and to give us the free gift of eternal life.

If God gave his love for me freely, not based on my performance, shouldn't I do the same for my kids?

Thanks again, Dad, for showing me, through you, my heavenly Father's eternal, unconditional love.

And please know that I did always try to do my best, at least partly because I always saw you doing your best to please your Father in heaven.

I tried my best because your unconditional love motivated it within me.

It may be the greatest and most important gift you ever gave me.

"God bless you!"

■

D efining moments. Everyone has them. When one's father recognizes such a moment, it's especially meaningful.

My pilgrimage to enter ministry was long and arduous. From my earliest moments, I can vividly remember people saying, "You're going to be just like your dad." In fact, I remember a snapshot of me at the age of eleven or so, Dad's hat on my head, his briefcase in one hand, his Bible in the other. That picture only further etched in people's minds that I was going to be like Dad.

Yet I also vividly remember the nights Dad would come home fatigued after a fifteen-hour day. I remember the pointed barbs from cynical church people that hurt him and perhaps hurt my mother even more. Ministry? It wasn't on my radar screen.

But the Hound of heaven finally captured my heart. I eventually knew God's ultimate plan, before the world was even created, was for me to be in ministry. I entered seminary in 1980.

For four years I tenaciously labored to complete my master of divinity and doctor of ministry degrees. In June 1980, I accepted the call to the Forest Hill Church in Charlotte, North Carolina.

Several days before my first sermon, Dad sent me a letter. I have always felt that it was one of the absolute high points of my life. Indeed, every time I've read it over the last twenty-plus years (which has been often; it stays in my desk drawer), I've experienced the same warmth I felt in late June, 1980.

Let me share it with you now:

June 26, 1980

Dear Son,

First, let me say I hope this is not too late to reach you prior to Sunday morning. I have allowed the time slip up on me beyond what I had anticipated.

Second, there would not be sufficient time now, or in the near future even, to begin to set down all the myriad thoughts that clamor in my alleged mind even at this moment.

I had to take just a moment, however, to address this note which I pray will reach you prior to your first Sunday in your first pastorate. Of course this is not the first service you have ever conducted, or the first sermon you have ever preached, or, indeed, the occasion of your actual ordination into the ministry and Installation into your first pastorate.

It is, however, that first time when you as the prospective pastor meet together with those people who have called you in your worship of Almighty God and of His Son, our Lord and Savior, and the Great Head of the Church. IN THAT SENSE THIS OCCASION IS UNIQUE AND OF UTMOST IMPORT.

As one who along with your beloved mother has been among those closest to you over the years, and who has rejoiced and cried with you as you climbed life's peaks and trudged its valleys, as you have sailed through sunlight and trudged through tears, in spirit I will stand with you Sunday morning as you proclaim, "Let us worship God." Your mother will join me as we throw a curtain of prayer around you and those people with whom you serve. You face a future where your heart will thrill at victories in Christ and throb at frustrations. In both, the same Lord will stand with and by you to steady your step. With your dear Marilynn you will join heart and hand in sharing this life together in Christ.

So . . . all thanks be to God, my son, Who has called you to this glorious ministry and to our Lord Jesus Christ in and through Whom all things are possible. Only believe in and trust Him! God bless you!

All my love,

Dad

Fathers, mothers, relatives, friends, please hear this: Significant moments in your relatives' and friends' lives can be greatly and forever enhanced by a simple letter acknowledging the defining moment and interpreting it through your life's lens for the future. You can help shape an entire life, an entire career, a troubled time, with your written words.

Don't miss this opportunity! It may well never come again.

My Dad knew the power of positive words during a defining moment. It has forever affected my life in a positive way.

I hope it will yours, too.

And especially your loved ones who need you and your wisdom during life's . . .

Defining moments.

Part Three

Personal Counsel

"My father just died."

We were in Kansas City. We had moved there from Charlotte in the early sixties. I was just a teenager, trying to adjust to a new city, a new life.

It was early in the morning. I was sound asleep when Dad quietly entered my room. He gently sat on the side of the bed. He caressed my forehead and slowly awakened me.

He whispered in my ear, "My dad died last night. I must return to North Carolina. I'll be gone a few days. I love you."

He didn't leave for a few moments. You need to know that until this moment, I had never seen my dad cry. But he started to cry now. Tears slowly moved down his cheek. Then he left.

Dad was different after this moment. I can't exactly explain it. I don't totally understand. He was more tender and understanding. It wasn't a huge immediate change. But he changed. Tears were a bit easier. Sensitivity was a bit more evident.

Someone once said to me that a man doesn't really become a man until the death of his father.

That may have been what happened to Dad that day. I'm not sure what happened, but it was profound.

And I guess I still have some growing to do.

I don't look forward to the day.

*"Friends are like elevators.
They either take you up or they bring you down."*

■

We were living in Kansas City at the time. I was around fourteen years old. I found some friends in the neighborhood. They weren't my parents' favorite people, but for the most part my parents didn't object.

Then came that fateful family vacation in Colorado one summer. I didn't want to go. I wanted to stay with my friends and have fun. I saw a family vacation as a real downer, a drag, basically no fun at all.

I protested to my parents. I told them I didn't want to go. I informed them that one of my neighborhood friends had offered me the possibility of staying with him for the two weeks my parents would be gone. My Dad emphatically said, "No." It was stated in no uncertain terms. No debate was even allowed.

I protested even more loudly. A huge argument ensued. I became angrier with every protest. Dad stood steadfast. He tolerated my adolescent diatribe but stood his ground. I went on the family vacation. Frankly, I had a good time, but I wouldn't let my parents know it at the time.

Upon return to Kansas City I was shocked to discover that my friends had gotten into a lot of trouble. One night, they had all sneaked out of their houses. The friend with whom I would have stayed had his driver's license. He took his parents' car and picked up everyone else. On an isolated street, they pried some hubcaps loose and stole them. A neighbor saw them and called the police, and they were soon picked up and arrested. They were handcuffed and fingerprinted. It was humiliating for their parents. It was the talk of the neighborhood for months to come.

You see where I'm going, don't you? Had I been there, too, I would have been arrested and subjected to all their humiliation. I would have embarrassed my mom and dad.

After arriving home and hearing the news, I went into the den one night and sheepishly apologized to my mom and dad for the way I'd behaved. I actually told them I'd enjoyed the family vacation.

Dad thanked me for my apology. Then he said, "Son, always remember that friends are like elevators. They either take you up or they bring you down."

That's a lesson I've never forgotten.

I hope my kids won't either.

"Remember whose and who you are."

■

I didn't date a lot in high school. I thought I was too tall and gawky for anyone to have much interest. Occasionally, however, I gathered the courage to ask a girl out.

I would put on my finest garb in preparation for the date. I even splashed a few drops of Brut on the cheeks and neck to make a positive impression.

Then, as I was leaving, Dad would always say the same thing.

"Son," he'd say, "Always remember whose and who you are."

At first I didn't have a clue to what he was referring. Through the years, the dense fog of my mind has begun to clear.

He was simply adjuring me to remember whose I am, to whom I belong. I am God's child. I belong to him. He created me. I am his. Ultimately I am accountable to him for all my actions. Indeed, he is my invisible partner wherever I am, whatever I do. Therefore, Dad was reminding me that I needed to act like a child of God with my date.

Moreover, he was reminding me who I am. I am David Chadwick. My last name is my dad's last name. When I am in public, I need to remember I am not only representing myself, but also representing my dad. Whatever I do ultimately reflects on him. He wanted me to remember this truth.

I have never forgotten whose and who I am.

Understanding this truth affected my dating life.

Actually, it has affected my entire life.

In fact, Dad recently sent me the following poem. It has been something by which he lives.

Your Name

You got it from your father.
It was all he had to give.
So it's yours to use and cherish,
For as long as you may live.

If you lose the watch he gave you,
It can always be replaced.
But a black mark on your name, Son,
Can never be erased.

It was clean the day you took it,
And a worthy name to bear.
When he got if from his father,
There was no dishonor there.

So make sure you guard it wisely,
After all is said and done.
You'll be glad the name is spotless,
When you give it to your son.

(Edgar Albert Guest, 1881–1959)

*"Reasonable people know somewhere
there must be a ceiling."*

It absolutely startled the sports world in the late 1960s. Jake Gibbs, a college catcher, signed a contract with the New York Yankees for an amazing one hundred thousand dollars. No one could believe it—an unproven college athlete now earning six figures.

I decided to write a paper for a high school English class on the subject. I did extensive research and then sat down and wrote the paper. I thought it was a very good analysis of the situation.

I gave it to Dad to read.

He told me he really liked it. He confirmed I had done a good job on my research. He then asked if he could help me re-write the conclusion. He said I was fine on description but a little short on prescription.

I was eager for his help.

He only added one sentence: "Reasonable people know somewhere there must be a ceiling."

That phrase became the theme sentence of my paper. I stated it and restated it. My teacher loved it. I received an A.

I wonder what would happen if I wrote it today?

Recently, several high school athletes entered the NBA draft. They were all taken in the top ten. They were guaranteed approximately ten million dollars over the next three years. A top baseball pick recently received even more.

Are there any reasonable people left?

Not even Dad saw this one coming.

A gross over-infatuation with sports was one the major reasons Gibbon cited for the fall of the Roman Empire in his book *The Decline and Fall of the Roman Empire.*

God help us all.

*"When you're late, you're
stealing other people's time."*

■

I can still see Dad in the car, impatiently waiting for everyone to pile in. He was always terribly frustrated whenever we were late.

It became like a mantra for him. As we pulled out of the driveway, he would always say, "Kids, don't you understand? Whenever you're late, you are stealing other people's time."

Then he would continue, "Would you steal their money?" We'd always answer, "No, sir."

"Well," he would then say, "would you steal their cars? Or their houses?"

We would always answer "No, sir."

Then would always come the punch line: "Then why are you so haphazard about stealing their time?"

We never had an answer. We didn't need one. Dad had made his point.

To this day I become antsy whenever I'm late. I even had one young staff-person tell me he thought I had a fetish about always being on time!

I don't think it's a fetish. I think it's respect, especially for other people who have the same hours and minutes in a day that I have. And when I make them wait, I honestly think I'm stealing their time.

I wouldn't steal their money, or their cars, or their houses.

I think you know what I'm saying.

But I learned it first from my Dad.

Blame him.

He's the one who taught it to me.

And I'm very grateful.

"There is a huge difference between your wants and needs."

nterestingly, I never grew tired of Dad's stories about life during the Depression. It was a life to which I could not relate but nevertheless found fascinating.

I couldn't know what it was like for my father to stand in line all day long, almost begging for a job. I couldn't understand what it was like for my father to lose his job and go from job to job, hoping to bring pennies home. I couldn't know what it was like to stand in line for hours for a job, only to hear nothing was available, come back tomorrow. I couldn't know what it was like to wonder if food would be on the table at night. If there was food, sometimes it was simply a bowl of soup. I couldn't know what it was like not to be able to play sports because you were needed at home immediately after school to work in the fields and around the house. Everyone had to do a fair share. I couldn't know what it was like to walk for miles to school. I couldn't know what it was like to have just one set of clothes. I couldn't know what it was like to lose your mother when you were twelve, the parent to whom you were most attached because Dad was gone looking for work. I couldn't know what it was like to have all your Christmas presents made, not bought, because you couldn't afford any. I couldn't know what it was like to have eight people living in three rooms, constantly bumping into one another, having to wait for a long time to use the bathroom.

Yet this was Dad's life as a child. This is how he grew up.

Therefore, you can imagine his lack of patience with children who demanded material possessions. We would hound him. One of our favorite lines was, "But the Mitchells have it."

He would always lower his voice and simply say, "We're not the Mitchells."

However, there is the phrase I remember most from him when we kids would bother him about wanting more and more. It would always come after another inane phrase we would utter to him: "But Dad, I really need . . ."

He would always calmly and politely respond, "There's a huge difference between your wants and needs."

Whenever we would listen, he would then tell us about the Depression and what his life was like. Then he would also tell us how, during these tough times, God would always faithfully supply his and his family's every need. Not their wants, but their every need.

I don't think we listened to him very well. Then, it seemed like the endless meandering of a dinosaur from a forgotten era.

As I have aged, I've learned he's correct. I've also learned that my voracious wants are not very important after all.

And I've learned that perhaps my generation has missed the beauty of the struggle.

For it's in the struggle that faith is learned.

"The most important shot is the next one."

I see it in my daughter when she plays basketball. I see it in my older son, too. My youngest just enjoys the moment, and the seriousness of the game hasn't set in yet. I hope it never does.

To what am I referring? Our tendency, mine included, to hang our heads and sulk when we make a mistake on the floor. And while we're feeling sorry for ourselves, the other team is racing up court to score another basket. We're pouting, and the other team is succeeding.

Dad noticed this tendency in me when I played in high school. He finally confronted me with it. He told me it was useless, even senseless.

Then he said the phrase I'll never forget. "Son," he said, "the most important shot is the next one."

He's right. The past is the past. You can't drive your car down the freeway by constantly staring in the rear view mirror. If you do so, you're inviting an accident to occur immediately or your opponent to score an easy, quick basket.

Now, when I make a mistake, which often still happens, I've learned my lesson. I admit it—I own up to the mistake I made. I quit it—I try very hard not to make the same mistake twice. I forget it—I move on, refusing to dwell upon the mistake.

Why? Because the most important shot is the next one.

"Avoid the snare to compare."

When I was a high school basketball player in the 1960s in Orlando, Florida, I was hailed as one of the best big players ever to play in the area. I could not have been prouder to sign a letter of intent with the University of North Carolina, a regular national power.

During my freshman year at UNC, another big man burst onto the Central Florida scene. He was gathering local and national attention, even threatening a couple of the records I had set.

Home for Christmas, I decided to go watch this new phenom first hand. I sat through the entire game, critically assessing his play.

When I arrived home, Dad asked me about him. I shrugged my shoulders. We continued to talk about him. During the next hour or so, I must have said, "Ah, he's not that good," at least a dozen times, as my dad pointed out.

Finally, Dad quoted William Shakespeare, "Me thinks thou protesteth too much." Then he smiled.

He got me. I was enormously intimidated by this new guy. I couldn't enjoy my own successes. I had to tear him down to build myself up.

Finally, he simply said, "Son, avoid the snare to compare. It's a dead end street."

Does he have to be right most all the time?

"With every right, there is a responsibility."

At the end of my junior year in high school, I was selected to be a member of the first team, all-state basketball team. I was the sole junior. It was a great honor. Honestly, it was a total surprise to me. I had no idea I would make it. I remember jumping for joy in my parent's bedroom after my high school coach had called to tell them the news. A handprint rested on their ceiling for years to come as a joyous reminder of that night.

Because of this basketball notoriety, I was nominated to run for the senior class presidency. I was shocked. I didn't think I deserved this either. I had only been at the school for one year. I didn't see myself as a leader, just a skinny basketball player! Nevertheless, I agreed to run.

There was just one catch. I had to write and give a speech in front of the entire junior class before the election. At this point in my life, I was extremely shy. I still felt very tall and gawky. I had no confidence in writing and making this speech.

So I went to Dad. I begged for his help. After all, he had to do this speech-giving deal every week! So he sat down with me. We started writing it together.

"Dad," I finally said. "I think we need a key phrase. There needs to be something that grabs the listeners, something that addresses where kids today are. What do you think kids in 1966 need to understand? What do my contemporaries need to understand?"

"Son," he said, "in my opinion, your generation, above all else, needs to remember that with every privilege there is a responsibility."

That was the keynote of my speech. I said it in five different ways, over and over again.

I won in a landslide.

Today, as we've entered the twenty-first century, I wonder if Dad is a prophet. As I examine the self-absorption and self-aggrandizement of us Boomers, I'm certain all of us need to be reminded of Dad's commentary on us in 1966. "With every right there is a responsibility."

Good words for the most privileged generation ever.

"I'm sorry. I was simply wrong."

After my junior season in high school, it became apparent that I was going to receive a four-year college scholarship. Letters from all over the country started to arrive. I became very excited about my basketball future.

Stetson University near Orlando annually offered a camp to the top junior players in the state of Florida. The coach at Stetson personally contacted my high school coach and asked if I would attend.

There was just one catch. The camp cost one hundred dollars. NCAA rules required that my family pay the cost. So I went to Dad and asked if he would pay for the camp. After all, he obviously wouldn't have to pay a penny for my college education.

He told me he couldn't pay for the camp—it was too expensive. He said it was simply impossible for him to do so.

I was shocked. Finally, I told Dad to cash in a United States savings bond he had purchased for me at birth. Its value was approximately one hundred dollars.

I attended the camp and came home with my arms filled with trophies. I had been named best player, had the most points and rebounds, and was selected to the all-tournament team. It only heightened my reputation as one of the best players in the state. It only enhanced my recruitment.

And the moment I put the trophies on the case, Dad knew he had made a mistake. It was then he said to me, "I'm sorry, Son. I made a mistake. I should have sent you."

This gave me a chance to grow, too. You see, I had to stop and try to understand Dad's background. His childhood was so difficult that a hundred dollars seemed a small fortune. Even though he could have easily afforded to send me to the camp, the mere thought of spending a hundred dollars for a sports camp was incomprehensible. I grew by understanding him.

But the most significant lesson I learned from this interaction was that everyone needs to be ready to apologize, especially fathers. We dads are human and make mistakes.

Our children will make similar mistakes. They, too, need to learn how to say, "I'm sorry."

But they probably won't learn it if we don't teach them.

By actually saying the words so difficult for humans to utter:

"I'm sorry. Please forgive me."

"It had to be your decision."

■

The process for choosing a school to attend was gut wrenching. I was contacted by about 130 schools from all over the country. I visited eleven and narrowed that list to three: Florida, Vanderbilt, and North Carolina. It was a very difficult decision. All three were very attractive to me.

During the decision period, I would go to Dad over and over and ask, "What do you think I should do, Dad? Where do you think I should go?"

He would never answer. He would always shrug and say, "Where do *you* think you should go? It's entirely your decision."

I finally decided to attend North Carolina. I loved Dean Smith, its tradition, and future prospects for winning. Moreover, since I was originally from North Carolina, I already had a lot of family there. It's a decision I've never regretted.

After I had made the decision, I went to Dad and asked him to tell me where he thought I should have gone. Without batting an eye, he said, "Oh, North Carolina. That's where I always thought you should attend."

I was a bit frustrated. I went through all those months of agony; he had an opinion and never told me? I didn't get it, and I told him so.

"Son," he finally said, "I did think you should attend North Carolina. But it had to be your decision. It would be your responsibility. You had to own it. It had to be your decision."

I hate it when he does that.

But he was right, very right.

Today I thank him for it.

And I do the same thing to my kids!

(They don't like it either).

*"Keep an open mind, but don't
let your brains fall out."*

■

C ollege life is challenging for a lot of reasons. You're forced
to deal with life on your own for the first time. I vividly remember watching my parents drive away after depositing me
at my dormitory. I had to choke back tears.

You also have a real, live roommate to whom you're not related. If you leave your room a mess, or if you're going through
a bad mood, patience doesn't necessarily abound! Nor will the
roommate pick up after you.

However, probably the greatest challenge in university life
is professors and peers constantly challenging cherished beliefs.
Almost from the first day on campus, students are exhorted to
have an open mind about all subjects. Why is premarital sex
wrong? Why not use mind-enhancing and mind-expanding
drugs? Why not look at pornography? Who gave the gov-
ernment all this authority? Why can't we question parental
authority?

These "bull sessions," as they were commonly called, would often last into the wee hours of the morning. Point and counterpoint would be made. Each person would try to prove the other one wrong. We would argue to the point of exhuastion.

To suggest that profs and peers had absolutely no influence on my young impressionable mind would be, at best, sophomoric. In fact, I found some of my own views bending a bit, swaying in the winds of college public opinion.

One break, I went home to visit Mom and Dad. It was always fun to have down time, simply to rest and enjoy Mom's great meals. Over one of these meals, I began discussing some of my new "thoughts" on different subjects with Dad.

He listened politely, then offered a rebuttal. I responded with what I heard in the "bull sessions." He would answer, most often with something like, "Son, for hundreds of years Western Civilization has defined and refined morals, principles, and standards. Are you now saying that in order to help make society work best and for the common good, we should simply throw aside what good people have discovered to be true?"

"Dad," I remember responding, "I just want to have an open mind. I don't want to be bound by society's previous mistakes."

"I understand, David," he concluded. "And that's not altogether bad. We do need to correct past social wrongs and to be released from traditions where we continue to make horrific decisions. However, as you quest to have an open mind, please do me one favor: Don't let your brains fall out."

I've never forgotten that phrase. Keep an open mind, but don't let you brains fall out.

Someone once teased that a conservative is simply a liberal with a teenage daughter. I doubt that is entirely true, but having walked with my daughter through her teenage years, and having observed a culture slowly losing its values and principles, I understand the feeling. I wonder if many of our cultural educators and leaders, in a quest for open-mindedness, have let truth slide to the wrong side.

My Dad thinks they have.

He's very progressive on issues that involve human rights. But he won't yield on bedrock convictions of personal morality and needed social mores.

In other words, he has an open mind, but his brains are still very much assembled!

Sounds like a balance I greatly desire in my own life.

I hope you do too.

"A good carpenter doesn't blame his tools."

I didn't get to play a great deal my sophomore year at UNC. I was young, weak, and not as skilled as the other players.

There was only one problem. I thought I was as good as they were. I was a hotshot high school player and had played well on the freshmen team. I therefore thought I should receive more playing time than I actually did.

I considered transferring to another school to complete my final two years of college eligibility. I wanted to play. I thought I was a good player. Therefore, playing time was my right and privilege.

I shared with Dad my thoughts. He was reading the paper at the time. He put it down and pondered my statements for a moment. As usual, he asked the most important and poignant question: "Why don't you think you received the playing time you think you deserved?"

I began to list the reasons I'd concluded over the months: The coaches weren't being fair; they had preferences and favorites; they didn't give me a chance. He calmly listened.

Finally, he spoke. "You know, David," he said, "a good carpenter doesn't blame his tools." He then picked up his newspaper and started reading it again.

I'd heard him previously utter this phrase to me. It was during my senior year in high school.

The team had been rated preseason the third best team in the state. We had three starters returning from a championship team. I had been selected first team all-state the previous season. I was the only junior on the team. We were certain a state championship was within our grasp.

That is, until the first two games of the season. We traveled to South Florida and played two outstanding teams to open the season. We were handily defeated in both games. Disappointment is not a strong enough word to describe our feelings.

We returned to Orlando. Not one of us, especially me, wanted to go to classes on Monday. At every corner, we heard the question, "What went wrong? I thought you guys were supposed to be really good!"

Dad overheard me talking to a teammate that night, trying to answer all the questions people were asking us. He heard me offering the usual reasons. The guards didn't play very well. We weren't really prepared. Maybe it was the coaches. On and on I went playing the blame game. I was finding every one else to blame, casting reasons for our disappointment on others.

After I hung up the phone, Dad put down the newspaper he was reading. Our eyes caught one another. There was a moment of uncomfortable silence. Finally, he simply said,

"You know, Son, a good carpenter doesn't blame his tools." Then he picked up his newspaper and started reading again. Nothing more was said. He had made his point.

The truth is I had played very poorly. The truth is I wasn't accepting responsibility for my own poor play, for my contribution to the two losses. From that moment onward, I refused to say anything negative about anyone else, looking only at my own failures within the team context. Amazingly, I started playing better, and so did the team!

Through the years I've always been uncomfortable with the victim mentality pervasive in American culture. It seems that everyone loves to blame their own bad choices and mistakes on everyone else! Indeed, today, I must confess increasing irritability at people's refusal to accept responsibility.

I don't go as far as saying, "If it's going to be, it's up to me!" This maxim doesn't take seriously enough our interdependence on one another. At times, we do hurt one another, and our pain is not our fault. I can't prevent some bad things happening to me.

However, I can choose my response when bad things happen to me. At that moment, I can choose to respond with hope and not despair, with faith and not blame. I can choose to look within and see my own areas of weakness. I can choose to start making choices that help, not hinder, my growth in life.

After all, a good carpenter doesn't blame his tools.

And I do want to be a *good* carpenter, not a mediocre one.

Is there really another option?

*"Shoot for the stars. You may only arrive at the moon,
but you've never been to the moon before!"*

    ■

When I signed a scholarship to play basketball at the University of North Carolina, I had dreams of being an All-American and one day playing in the NBA. After signing the scholarship, I was amazed at how many people, some even friends, assailed my decision and told me I'd never play at UNC.

I sought Dad's counsel on how to handle their criticism. It was beginning to wound my hopes and dreams.

He simply responded, "Shoot for the stars. You may only arrive at the moon, but you've never been to the moon before!"

I did. I worked hard toward my dream. Guess what? I didn't reach the stars. I wasn't an All-American. I didn't play in the NBA. But I did get to play at UNC. I started eleven games as a senior. I even scored thirty points in one game. I received and signed a European contract and played there for three years. I played for Dean Smith, a truly great man and arguably the greatest college coach ever.

No, I didn't reach the stars. But I got to the moon, and the view was truly spectacular. Indeed, I had never been to the moon before!

Why? Because I know I did my best.

I know I fervently pursued my dreams.

I also know the joy was actually in the journey, not the destination.

However, the moon is a nice place to be. I'd never seen it before. And without the dream of the stars, I would never have visited it.

I hope to see you there some time!

"Don't listen too closely when people jeer or cheer."

■

I was playing in my first year of professional basketball in Ostend, Belgium. It was the first game of the season. Everyone in the town and on the team was excited to see how good we could be. We were playing one of the best teams in the country. It would be an acid test for our team.

I played one of the best games I've ever played. I scored thirty-four points, had a dozen rebounds or so, and was simply unstoppable. The city cheered my success. I was on the front page of the local newspaper. Everywhere I went people would stop me and congratulate me on my success. I didn't have to buy one meal that week. Everyone was very excited about me and the team!

The next week we played a team about thirty miles down the road. They were archrivals. The people from Ostend flooded the gym to watch their team and the new hero on the team, me.

We lost. I played terribly. I couldn't have played worse. I scored six points or so, and my rebounding was totally neutralized. I went home that evening totally discouraged. Few, if any, even spoke to me. I went from hero to goat in one week. Plus, I purchased all my meals that week! It was extremely embarrassing.

I called home during that week. Dad answered. I told him about the high of the week before and the low I was presently experiencing. I sought some advice.

He gave it to me. He simply said, "Son, people are fickle. They change opinions daily. Don't listen to their opinions." Or, put differently, there is a phrase I learned indirectly from Dick Bennett, the former head basketball coach at the University of Wisconsin. His son Tony became my close friend when he played for the Charlotte Hornets and shared it with me. Here's what his dad taught him: "Don't listen too closely when people cheer or jeer."

It's been an important truth for me to learn through the years. Whether it has been basketball, academics, church work, radio outreach, whatever—you're only as good in people's eyes as your last success. People are fickle. For that reason, I've been forced to develop an internal thermostat to regulate my emotions based on God's love for me, not people's acceptance or rejection.

Because one day they'll love you. And the next day they may hate you.

But God's love lasts forever, amidst the cheers and the jeers.

"Always remember to diet and exercise."

D ad was diagnosed as a borderline diabetic some twenty plus years ago. The disease could be controlled, but only through diet and exercise.

Soon thereafter, Dad sat me down and warned me that diabetes can often be hereditary. He shared with me the potential damage to my body if I didn't take care of my own diet and exercise.

"I wish I had started sooner," he confessed. "Always remember to diet and exercise."

Today, Dad's in his eighties. He walks every day. He watches what he eats. He's in great health. And the older I become, the more meaningful this counsel becomes.

I often wonder how many mental, emotional, and physical problems could be overcome if we simply watched our diets and committed to exercise on a regular basis. I know these simple facts: When I exercise and watch my diet, I lose weight. I feel more energy. My moods are more positive. Depression doesn't sink me into deep, dark holes.

If Dad's an example of its benefits, we all should follow his example.

And his advice.

Always remember to diet and exercise.

Oh, by the way.

I am.

"The enemy of the best is the good."

■

As the church I oversee has continued to grow, all kinds of offers come my way. This organization wants me to speak here. This board would like for me to serve there. People come to me with variations on the same theme, "God loves you, and *I* have a wonderful plan for your life."

Nature abhors a vacuum. If there's emptiness, something will try to rush in and fill it.

How then does one decide priorities? How does one decide what is most important among all the different requests for your time?

Dad encouraged me from the earliest days of my ministry to know my purpose, both personally and ecclesiastically. He knew I needed a clear mission that could be easily and immediately stated when asked.

He told me that during World War II, an MP would have the responsibility to stop a soldier found walking around with no apparent purpose and to ask him, "What is your mission?"

If the person couldn't immediately respond, the MP could forcibly detain him.

Dad pushed me to know my own purpose personally and ecclesiastically. It would help in defining not only what needed to be done, but also what didn't need to be done immediately, if at all.

In fact, one of Dad's favorite phrases was, "The enemy of the best is the good."

Good things always beckon our time. They'll fill up any vacuum. But are they the best? You can't answer that question until you know what the best is.

That's why everyone needs to know and be able to state clearly and succinctly his or her life purpose. They need to know why on earth they are here.

Once defined, you can almost always choose the best. You can stay focused on your calling, your purpose, and your objective in life.

In turn, once you let go of the many good things that aren't your best, others can pick them up. One of those good things may be *their* best!

More objectives are realized. People don't become burned out. More people are satisfied with what they do.

I think that's what Dad was trying to teach me on that day long ago.

*"Tears are God's way of keeping
a head from becoming big."*

When I had made some unwise decisions about transitioning the church, I was forced one Sunday to go before the congregation and apologize. Believe me, it wasn't fun. Eating humble pie before more than a thousand people was not my idea of a picnic. But I knew I had to do it. Mistakes had been made, primarily by me. Therefore, it was I who needed to make the official apology and communicate the church's direction in the future.

I'll never forget that day. It was gray and cold. I'd spent an hour in prayer, seeking internal, indeed eternal, help. I went before the congregation, shared the history of the problem, and apologized for my mistakes. I then shared how the leadership and I were going to correct the plan, and I asked for the people's patience.

Then it happened. It even caught me by surprise. I don't know where it came from.

I started to cry. I was truly repentant. It wasn't a show meant to manipulate. It was pure, unadulterated sadness.

I finally finished the talk and left the platform. I was humiliated. I had let down my emotions. I was certain that people now perceived me as weak. I knew I had lost my leadership role. I was completely convinced they could never follow me again after this raw, emotional outburst.

Later that evening, I called Dad and shared with him what had happened. He listened intently. Then he shared with me how he also had broken down and cried in front of his leadership. However, he told me that it wasn't a negative for his leadership. Indeed, he discovered that it helped his leadership. People saw him as more human, more real, more approachable. Then he told me how he hoped the same would occur for me. He said he had wished Richard Nixon had sincerely apologized in the early 70s. He said he was convinced even our large nation would have quickly forgiven him.

Finally, he concluded his conversation with these words, "Besides, tears are God's way of keeping a head from becoming big."

Dad was exalting servant leadership. He was simply saying that a humble leader who is real is respected. Arrogant, big-headed leaders don't motivate people to follow. They cause suspicion.

Indeed, the next day my office was flooded with calls from people thanking me for my honesty, openness, and humanity.

They said it made them want to follow me even more! Not only did we make it through the transition over the next year, but I'm convinced my leadership was solidified for years to come.

All because of a few tears.

A few tears that prevented me from getting the big head.

"Never retire. Just re-fire."

D ad was pastor of a three thousand-member church in
Orlando, Florida. He had huge responsibilities among
some of the city's most influential and powerful people.

As he passed the sixty-year mark, he knew it was rapidly becoming time for him to leave. Some counseled him to consider
retirement. He did, but not as most people would. He looked at
people who had performed great Christian service through the
centuries. He examined the Bible and its major people of faith.

He could not find one person who ever retired. He saw no
Christian pattern of working until you're sixty-five and then
retiring. It may do for horses, but not ministers.

It was at this point in his ministry that an organization
called the Outreach Foundation approached. It was a fledgling
organization in his denomination committed to raising money
for home and world missions.

Dad felt the call. He left First Presbyterian and poured himself into his new job. Over the next years, literally millions of
dollars were poured into a variety of worldwide needs. Because

of his efforts, the poor were clothed, housed, and fed. New churches were built. People's lives were given hope and meaning. God's unconditional love was powerfully proclaimed.

He told me these were probably the most satisfying years of his entire ministry.

Personally, I had never seen Dad happier or more fulfilled.

During this time, when he talked about this new calling, he loved to tell the story of the very gifted minister who was being wooed by a large corporation to leave the ministry and use his outstanding gifts for them. The boss of the corporation asked what it would take. The minister said it wasn't about money. The boss began to quote figures that went skyward to six digits. Finally, the young minister said, "You don't understand. It's not about the money. Your job is simply too small. It's not big enough."

One day I asked, "When should someone retire?"

He simply responded, "Never retire. Just re-fire."

He did. Today, he is moving into his mid-eighties. He doesn't work for the Outreach Foundation anymore. He stopped that some years ago.

But he's still preaching almost every Sunday. He's doing it with fire, as if he's re-firing every week.

One day, I want to be like my dad.

"If the sun comes up, there's always hope."

I t was during one of those times in ministry when I was wondering if I would make it. They haven't happened often. Usually, I can wrestle them away with a couple days off or a good, long coffee break with my wife, Marilynn.

However, sometimes the full pressures of ministry converge. When this tsunami occurs, that's when I wonder if I can make it.

During one of those moments when gloom captured me, I went to Dad. I poured out my heart. I told him that I was engulfed in darkness. There seemed to be no hope in my soul. Every step felt like I was walking in quicksand, and each step made my legs feel increasingly fatigued. I didn't want to continue. I told Dad I felt totally hopeless.

With a twinkle in his eyes and sage counsel that only the years can give, he looked at me and calmly said, "David, don't feel hopeless. Don't ever feel hopeless. If the sun comes up, there's always hope."

That phrase has echoed in my ears for years. The tough times have continued to come. I've still experienced deep, dark nights of the soul.

But I always emerge on the other side. Why? Because the next day the sun always comes up. Indeed, every single morning since the last major crisis in my life, the sun has risen. Therefore, there is always hope. God is still seated on his throne. He is still active, alive, working, yes, working even in the worst circumstances for a purposeful future. The proof is the first blush of light that sprinkles itself against the shadowy night.

At no time did Dad's wise counsel mean more to me than the morning of September 12, 2001. The United States and, indeed, the world were numb with shock over the terrorist assaults in New York City and Washington, D.C. Thousands of lives had been lost. Gloom filled our psyches. We all felt hopeless and in despair. "When is the next strike going to come?" we kept asking ourselves. "How do you fight an enemy whose name you don't know, one who hides and lurks in shadows?"

WBT is Charlotte's most popular news and talk radio station. I do a weekly faith-and-values program and a daily spot entitled "A Minute of Hope." During times of national crisis, the program director asks me to come in and, hopefully, add insight and counsel for the listening audience. Bill White, the present program director, asked me to do so on the Wednesday morning after the Tuesday attack.

I was driving to the station just after six in the morning. Few cars were on the road. Darkness covered the city. A stunned silence held us.

My soul was aching; my heart hurting. What could I say to the tens of thousands of people who would be listening to me this morning? I felt, well, hopeless.

Suddenly, a deep, soft, resonant voice spoke. It was a voice. It wasn't God's voice but another one that I'd learned to listen to, love, and respect through the years. It was Dad's. It was unmistakably his voice.

And he simply said, "Son, as long as the sun comes up, there's always hope."

At exactly that moment the sun broke through the clouds. Light shattered the night, and the darkness fled. Eventually, the healing hope of a new dawn gave hope to me.

I shared this experience with the listeners that morning. Many later told me it helped their healing, and renewed hope stirred within them when they heard me speak Dad's words.

I hope it does the same for you, too.

Because there is hope. Believe it! God is still working in his world. He is still actively involved in running all matters on this side of eternity. He is even working tragedy into triumph, terror to trust, hollowness to hope.

Why believe it?

I just looked outside.

Yes, you guessed it.

The sun rose again this morning.

Therefore, no matter what you're going through, there's always hope.

Part Four

Relationships

"Give it the test of time."

■

Remember your first kiss? Wow, I do. I was a junior in high school. (Was I a late bloomer by today's standards? I hope not!) Anyway, she lit a fuse in my heart I'll never forget.

I came home starry-eyed, gazing into future horizons, imagining this girl by my side forever and ever. We were meant to be; at least that's what every hormone in my body was yelling.

The next day, Dad noticed my walking on air. I think I may have stumbled into a table or two. Sensing what was going on, he casually said, "Got bit bad, huh?"

"What are you asking?" I shot back.

"Oh, nothing," he responded. "I just remember the first time I got bit, too."

I pretended he was out to lunch, which was where I wished he had been at that moment. I was totally embarrassed.

Sensing my embarrassment, he began to walk away. But before he had left the room, he simply said, "Give it the test of time."

I knew what he was saying, but I didn't want to listen. I had given it the test of time—two hours with this girl the night before! How I hated it when he meddled in my affairs.

The relationship lasted one month. You heard me. One month. The feelings on both sides quickly fizzled. We were teenagers, after all.

But I've never forgotten Dad's advice. I even give it to couples contemplating marriage today. Give it the test of time. There is no greater way to see if a relationship will work. Only time reveals differences, disagreements, and incompatible lifestyles. Only time shows goals, directions, and dreams.

Give it the test of time.

I'm anxiously watching my children's "bites." When I see one, have I got something I want to say!

Whether they listen is another matter.

But maybe they'll remember for another time, another place, another relationship.

I pray such.

"Get so close he can't kick you."

It happened during Dad's first pastorate in Greensboro, North Carolina. There was a prickly personality in the church. He was always objecting to every new idea, constantly stirring controversy, and criticizing Dad behind his back.

How do you handle a difficult person? He was wearing Dad out. His constant negativism was fracturing this tiny church.

Being relatively young and inexperienced, Dad sought counsel. He went to a renowned lecturer at a conference he was attending and outlined the problem. He begged this famous churchman for wisdom to address this very difficult situation.

The old sage simply said to Dad, "Get so close to him he can't kick you."

Dad understood. He returned to Greensboro and went to the man. He told him he knew the two of them were having difficulties. But he wanted him to know how much he cared for him as a person. He wanted to know if there was anything he could do for him, any way he could serve him. Was there anything in his life he could share with Dad, any hurt Dad could try to help heal, for the church needed them to pull together instead of in opposite directions.

The man broke down and cried. He proceeded to tell Dad his myriad problems. He chronicled them one after another.

Dad soon realized something that greatly aided him in ministry and in life for years to come. If someone is miserable, there's probably a good reason. Put another way, Dad learned that hurt people hurt people.

Dad simply cared for this man. He built a bridge to his heart instead of shooting him down.

You know what happened? Later this man donated a rather large gift to the church. And what do you suppose it was for? To send Mom and Dad away for a few days for a much-needed vacation.

Dad got so close he couldn't kick him.

He also got so close the man could give him a check!

A really nice check.

Nice going, Dad!

"I try to understand their side."

The most painful part of Dad's ministry came in the late 1970s. Dad had experienced a successful ministry. However, there were a few influential and powerful people who thought his time should end.

Dad and Mom had planned a two-week trip to South Korea to observe some missions. Dad would also do some preaching. It was a trip they had anticipated for months.

Right before they left, Dad caught wind from a very close friend that something was amiss. He heard that a few dissatisfied church members wanted to oust him. They had another man available, a friend of theirs, whom they believed would better suit their needs.

Dad probed to find out more information, but no more was given. There were just rumors.

So Dad and Mom left. This was obviously a burden on his heart. Interestingly, he later told me he never told Mom about this conversation during their weeks in Korea.

I was stunned. If this had happened to me, I would have immediately told Marilynn—not for her sake, but for mine! I would have needed support.

When I asked Dad why he never shared it with Mom, his answer was concise, "I didn't want to ruin the trip for her."

Upon their return to Orlando, rumors became reality. There was indeed a hostile takeover in the works. These few but powerful people were trying quietly to influence the leadership to give Dad a vote of "no confidence." He would then be forced to leave. They would take control of a newly-formed search committee for a new pastor and get "their man" in.

I don't know when I've seen Dad more depressed. He was stunned that Christians would behave like this. His entire sense of well-being was threatened.

I was visiting home one weekend from seminary during this brouhaha. Dad was so despondent that he asked me to preach for him. I gladly agreed. Amazingly, one of the members of the opposition actually asked for a meeting with me before I preached. I agreed to meet with him.

In the meeting he encouraged me to ask Dad to step down. He said it was a fruitless fight. He said Dad could not win.

He underestimated my dad. Dad immediately called for a meeting of the Session, the governing body of the church. These fifty-plus men and women were the very ones the small group was trying to influence to give Dad a "no confidence" vote. Dad decided issues needed to be confronted. If, indeed, there was a sizable group of his leadership that wanted him gone, so be it. He would leave. But he would not allow back-room arm-twisting to decide who was going the lead the Lord's church.

The congregation was aware of the meeting. Many had heard the rumors. They packed the fellowship hall for the meeting. One elder was chosen to stand up, list evidences of Dad's fruitful ministry, and then ask for a vote of confidence in his future leadership.

The vote was taken. Only four people voted against it, the four members of this small group. The members of the congregation who were present gave Dad a standing ovation. His ministry there continued with success for several years.

Then came the call to become the Executive Director of the Outreach Foundation. As stated earlier, these years were the capstone of Dad's life and ministry, the years that yielded the most fruit.

Here is a question to think about. Would Dad have accepted this venturesome and challenging call had he not faced the adversity above? Was God preparing his future through this pain? As C. S. Lewis said, "God whispers to us in our pleasures . . . but shouts in our pain" (*The Problem of Pain*). Someone may intend us evil. But those who trust God's goodness and sovereignty know that God is somehow using our situations for good.

But here's the best part of the story, in my opinion. Those four people remained in the church. I personally had hoped they'd leave of their own accord. Or I hoped others would drive them out of the church.

Neither happened. They all remained.

And Dad kept reaching out to them. He included them in the work of the church. He took them out to lunch. He continued to build relationships with them. He got so close they could never kick him again!

Yet he was never bitter. He was never vengeful. He didn't hold a grudge.

They never apologized or asked for forgiveness from Dad.

Yet he gave them forgiveness.

I later asked him how he could do that. Why wasn't he bitter? Why didn't he hold a grudge? I'm convinced I would have!

He simply responded, "I tried to understand their side." He put himself in their position, with their convictions and beliefs, their loyalties, their life priorities, their life influences, and concluded that had he been in their shoes, he might have done the same thing.

He sought to understand, not to be understood.

And bitterness didn't wither his soul.

I'm trying, Dad, really trying, to get this one down.

I'm not there yet.

But I'm trying.

I really want to understand this one.

"They'll need a new pastor."

▪

The 1960s were turbulent years for Americans. We were caught in the crosshairs of change, not the least of which was racial inequality.

The church was not immune to this turbulence, especially the church Dad oversaw.

Some Americans long for what they call "the good old days," when America was faith-based and much simpler. Certainly there seemed to be a greater consensus regarding family and moral values. But I'm not convinced racial harmony enjoyed a good old day at all.

To what do we desire to return? Segregated water fountains? African-Americans eating at the back doors of restaurants? Sitting in the backs of buses? Segregated restrooms?

From my earliest days, I remember Dad having a heart for racial equality. But it had not been natural for him. He was raised in the segregated South. He regularly heard racial slurs. Perhaps it was how his faith informed his life. Perhaps it was simply a gift from God. Whatever the reason, Dad never accepted racial inequality and segregation.

His commitment was tested in the 1960s in Orlando. One of the strategies of African-Americans was to move to areas where segregation existed and join all-white churches, especially those with the city's most influential citizens. That was the profile of First Presbyterian, Orlando.

Dad and his leadership learned that an African-American gentleman had moved to Orlando with that expressed purpose. Dad knew it was going to happen, but he didn't know what the response of his people would be.

I remember sitting around the dinner table, Dad sharing with all of us what was going to happen. He also shared how he was going to support his membership. He was going to take a public stand, if necessary, to express his commitment to the church's desire for racial equality.

I sheepishly asked, "Dad, what happens if the people don't accept him? What happens if the leadership and congregation reject your stand?"

I'll never forget his answer. He simply responded, "They'll have to find a new pastor."

The man did join. There was not much of an upheaval. A few of the prejudiced people in the church objected. A few stopped coming to church.

But the vast majority supported Dad's stand. A few other African-Americans later joined.

I can't remember a day I ever felt prejudiced. My athletic enterprises brought many deep and meaningful relationships.

Here's another way Dad's life shaped my own. I'm exceedingly grateful he fought the demons of his own time and culture. I'm very thankful that he taught me with his words and actions this basic truth:

All God's children are created equal.

Can't we all please drive this one deep into our hearts?

Please?

"Beware of dream killers."

◼

Jesus had a dream, a vision for his life. He was to go to Jerusalem. He would then be arrested. He would die on a cross to forgive us of our sins. That's why he came to this earth. It was his reason for being here.

Interestingly, right after Jesus' pronouncement, Peter, supposedly one of Jesus' closest friends, if not his closest, chimed in, "You can't do that." And he proceeded to try and prevent Jesus from going. Jesus' close friend tried to keep the dream from occurring. He was basically a dream killer.

When I signed a scholarship with the University of North Carolina, I was convinced that was where God wanted me. It was a long, difficult decision. But when I became convinced, I was really convinced.

Amazingly, over the next several weeks, I had person after person plant seeds of doubt in my mind. I'm sure some were well-intentioned. But they were dream killers.

Dad warned me they would come. He shared with me Jesus' experience with Peter.

I'm glad he did. The dream killers have kept coming through the years.

But, like Jesus, I've kept my eyes on the dream. I've kept focused on the vision.

His was the salvation of the world.

Mine is simply to love and serve him and to be a friend to spiritual seekers, those who are seeking to love and serve him.

That's my life's passion.

I hope God is pleased.

"The more you stir manure, the more it stinks."

I

f I could change one part of me, it would be my defensiveness. Since I can remember, whenever I received criticism,
from childhood to this very moment, I have tended to arch my
back and return the attack.

It's not a great characteristic if you're leading people in
ministry. In fact, one of my close work associates, who came
from a secular industry to join me in ministry over a decade
ago, aptly described the difference between dealing with people
in the workplace and dealing with those in ministry. He said,
"In the workplace people have strong opinions. In ministry,
they have divine truth."

When people state contrary opinions to mine, they are
most often saying, "God wants this done!" When I don't respond the way they desire, they become increasingly angry with
me. Unfortunately, my defensiveness too often kicks in. As a result, no one wins and everyone loses.

After a few years of exasperating ministry confrontations, I went to Dad for advice. I was fatigued about my defensiveness and the battles that ensued. I was tired of my immovable object attitude meeting the irresistible force of my critics' attitudes. Frankly, I didn't know if I could last in ministry. I therefore sought Dad's counsel.

His answer resonates in my mind even today. "Son," he said, "always remember this truth. The more you stir manure, the more it stinks."

It's a rather graphic analogy, but it's one that has helped set me free from most of my defensiveness (but not all—hey, no one's perfect!). Dad was simply saying that the more I stirred the controversy with my defensiveness, the more antipathy I was going to have returned to me. Conversely, if I refused to stir the problem with my defensiveness, the stink would eventually go away.

And that's what I've decided to do over the last several years. When the criticism comes, and it always does no matter what position I take, I simply say, "Thanks for the feedback," discern what truth may be there, change what needs to be changed, and then let it go.

Granted, if I don't change what my critic desires, I am then criticized for ignoring people when they offer me criticism! But I've come to realize that although I can't control the criticism coming to me, I can control my response to the criticism.

And I've decided not to respond by stirring the manure with my innate defensiveness. Why?

It doesn't work.

It only heightens emotions on both sides.

And the result always stinks.

Always.

And it *really* stinks.

Plus, it's not worth the battle.

"Dogs only bark at moving cars."

L et me share with you another area of criticism that I've had to try to overcome, one that occurs when I get a vision for what can happen, become creative with the vision's implementation, and then go for it. Inevitably, criticism abounds.

I was raised in the formal, traditional, liturgical church. I sometimes wonder if I were a kid today if I wouldn't be diagnosed with ADD. My mind, even as a child, would always be wandering from one idea to the next. Bottom line: It was hard for me to pay attention, especially to something slowly-paced that bored me.

That's what Sunday morning worship was for me. At the church my dad pastored in Charlotte, North Carolina, between 1953 and 1963, there is a pew about five rows back from the front on the right side with around forty pencil holes bored into the wood. You guessed it. I did it. Guilty as charged! I couldn't wait for the service to end. When Dad finally pronounced the benediction, I would sigh and think, "Thank goodness, I don't have to do this for another week!"

Therefore, I ran away from God's call to the ministry for many years. One reason, if not the reason, was that I thought the church was boring and irrelevant to the culture in which I lived. I never would have invited one of my friends to church for fear that he would fall asleep in worship.

Finally, when God caught me in 1976 in Gainesville, Florida, I relented to the sense of call but also whispered to him, "OK, I'll do this to which I know you've called me. But Lord, please don't let me bore people on Sundays like I was bored."

Perhaps this background will help you understand why, over the twenty-plus years I've been in local church leadership, I've invited change into the church. I've refused to live by the seven last words of the church: "We've never done it that way before." I've realized that the world is rapidly changing around us. Although the message of the church can never change, our methodologies must. And now I'm not hesitant to invite a friend to church! Even Dad attends the church I lead. He sometimes says to me, "Well, Son, it's not what I'm used to, but it's reaching people and for that I'm grateful and can support you."

You can well imagine how my leadership has fared in an institution that tenaciously clings to structures four to five hundred years old. Criticism has regularly come my way. People have not always appreciated my vision. The criticism has, at times, abounded.

However, much praise has also come my way. The church is on the cutting edge of reaching postmodern, unchurched people. We've grown tremendously over the twenty-plus years of my leadership, especially among those who felt as I did that the church was boring and irrelevant. Therefore, I've consistently lived in the tension of success and criticism.

At one point the criticism amidst my success overcame me. I therefore went to Dad. I asked him how I could handle the criticism. Could he help make sense of it for me? I was especially hurt from the fervent criticism from leaders in other churches. I remember saying to Dad, "I thought they were supposed to be on my team."

Dad didn't hesitate in his response. He simply said, "Dogs only bark at moving cars."

He is so right! No one ever criticizes something that isn't moving ahead.

Most change invites criticism. People prefer comfort. Moreover, when something becomes successful, it often threatens those who are afraid to change or who are stuck in their own ways.

Therefore, Dad suggested to me that criticism could be the greatest compliment I ever receive! It means I'm moving forward. Something positive is happening in my leadership. The car is not parked. It's moving ahead!

And when this happens, expect the dogs to run out, bark, and chase the car.

Expect it, Dad told me.

I have.

Interestingly, it has lessened the bite of the critics' comments.

After all, has anyone ever erected a statue to a critic?

Dad didn't give me that one.

But he could have.

*"Don't look at what you've lost
but what you've got left."*

W hen you're leading an innovative, creative organization, the critics not only come out and criticize, but
eventually, if you don't give them what they want, they leave
the organization! It's their ultimate trump card. It's most often
done with a grandiose departure that informs everyone else
they're leaving.

In the early 1990s, I moved the church I pastor toward a
more focused outreach. The transition was painful. Some, in-
cluding friends, were angry and very critical of me. I listened to
their concerns but didn't give them what they wanted. I knew
the vision. I stuck to it.

They then threatened to leave. I couldn't yield. One friend
even suggested I needed counseling because I was "obsessed
with the vision." A fairly sizable number of people left. It was
painful. I had to say good-bye to several close friends.

I went to Dad for counsel and comfort. My soul was
wounded. I kept seeing the faces of those who had left.

Whenever I saw them publicly, I winced. I continually concentrated on my losses.

Dad's response has remained prominent in my mind to this day. "Son," he said, "don't look at what you've lost, but what's left."

He knew the reality that you can't change the past. You can't control what others think of you. But you can take the positive that's left in your life and begin to build again.

That's what I did. I took the hundreds who didn't leave, who had committed to the vision and my leadership, and began to build again.

Amazingly, within months, the couple of hundred who had left were replaced with several hundred people, mostly consisting of the people we were trying to reach with the new vision! Within a few years, they had been replaced with a couple of thousand!

God is a God of the moment. He is building the present for his future. The past is the past. It can't be changed. But there's always something left in the rubble upon which a new foundation could be built.

In my life and leadership, it's one of the most important lessons I've ever learned.

Many, many thanks for giving me this one, Dad.

It's helped me in more ways than you'll ever know.

*"The grass may seem greener on the other side,
but it still needs to be mowed."*

■

During the time when the church was in crisis and people and friends were leaving, I received an inquiry from another church. It was a very large church in another part of the country with tremendous potential.

Marilynn and I began exploring it. It seemed like the right time to move. I could escape the pain. Plus, my leadership could be used in an even greater way in another large city.

Yet, after my second visit to this church, I felt uneasy. So did Marilynn. We could receive no peace in our sense of call.

I went to Dad. I explained the entire scenario. I desperately yearned for his wisdom.

He intently listened. He asked several questions as he always did. He probed my damaged emotions, my sense of call, my most inward motivations. He carefully listened as I explained the opportunity to transition a large church into a huge church.

After all the questions and answers, he paused and pondered. Finally, he said, "David, the grass may seem greener on the other side, but it still has to be mowed."

I declined the call. I would have accepted it for all the wrong reasons.

Moreover, I learned that the person who did accept the call after me only lasted a year. He followed someone who had been there for over thirty years, and he didn't meet everyone's expectations.

I wouldn't have made it either. As someone once said to me about the North Carolina coaching position, "I wouldn't want to be the person who follows Dean Smith as the head basketball coach at UNC. I would want to be the person who follows the person who follows Dean Smith."

The grass may seem greener on the other side, but it does still have to be mowed. Dad was correct about this truth. Moreover, in retrospect, I realize another truth, too. Sometimes that green grass is growing over a septic tank!

Thanks, Dad, for teaching me perseverance through tough times and contentment with what I have.

In the long run, the grass here has grown and grown . . . and become greener and greener.

I shudder to think what I would have missed had I not listened to Dad's wise counsel.

"Choose your battles wisely."

■

One of the highest-risk vocations is ministry. Believe it or not, many ministers, having lasted five years or less in the ministry, give up their sense of call and enter secular jobs.

I'm presently in my second decade of ministry. As I've already written, my years in ministry have not been without difficulty. I've had my fair share of critics and people angry with my leadership.

However, I've persevered. I've persisted amidst the pain. And I believe, with God's help, I'll finish strong.

How have I done it? How have I made it? I don't have a simple, easy formula, but one piece of counsel Dad gave me has probably helped me the most in my commitment.

During my first week of ministry back in 1980, I asked Dad if he could give me any counsel that might allow me to last.

Jokingly, he responded, "Well, as quickly as possible, become friends with the president of the women of the church and the church treasurer."

Then his smile disappeared. "Seriously, Son," he continued, "always, always choose your battles wisely. You only have so much psychological, spiritual, and emotional energy. Almost every day you'll be confronted with possible battles. Don't try to fight them all. You can't fight them all. Be careful. Choose your battles wisely."

Through the years, I've tried to follow this advice. When I'm confronted with a potential battle, I've always asked the question, "How important is this fight in the scheme of the entire vision? What will be the cost to me and to others? If I don't fight it, might it go away, its energy and attention dissipating naturally over time?"

By asking these questions based on Dad's wise counsel, I can guard my energy. I've seldom felt like giving up and leaving ministry because of a lack of inward reserves.

In essence, I've followed Dad's advice. It's some of the wisest counsel he's ever given me.

I'll never forget it.

As a result, I'm convinced I'll make it to the end. I'll run to the finish line of ministry.

Indeed, I'll finish strong!

"Be responsible, but don't take responsibility."

■

I'm the youngest child in my family. Howard and Carolyn, my older brother and sister, are wonderful people, but growing up they constantly challenged Mom and Dad. They caused my parents some heartburn now and then!

Growing up, I hated the conflict. Therefore, I decided not to cause my parents problems. I took on the label of the "good kid." I caused them a few problems, but not many. That was intentional on my part. Howard and Carolyn accused Mom and Dad of making me their favorite. They would always respond, "We love you all the same, but David simply doesn't give us the problems you give us."

I was a great kid to have around the house. However, as I've grown up, this desire to please followed me around like a yellow jacket sensing sugar on a hand. At times, it has become terribly painful, especially being a minister where criticism is commonplace. Moreover, whenever people would have problems, the "good kid" in me would rush to their aid, assume the problem, and become exhausted.

Dad gave me counsel that has helped me battle this problem. When he once saw me burdened with so many people's problems, unable to solve them, he simply said to me, "Son, be responsible, but don't take responsibility."

It's some of the best counsel he has ever given me. I still try to help people. I try to be responsible in helping others with their life's dilemmas. However, I steadfastly refuse to take responsibility for their problems. If they try to give it to me, I give it back. Ultimately, I know only they can solve their lifes' issues. I'll help. But I won't assume responsibility.

Interestingly, more people get well with this approach.

And it protects my energy level.

Thanks again, Dad.

"Always treat people the right way. You never know when you may need them to help you!"

■

Dad always taught me never to burn bridges. Getting so close to people that they couldn't kick you was always the best course, he said.

Beyond this truth, however, he also taught the value of always caring for people. You would never know how this treatment might positively affect your life or someone you know and care about.

This truth recently became a reality for me, and at first I didn't even know it.

My first cousin, Lou Ann, lives in Winston-Salem, North Carolina, with her husband Jeff, a very successful lawyer. They have several children. Their oldest son's name is Jeff Chadwick Wood. He just graduated from the University of North Carolina and decided to enter medical school. He applied to one of the most respected medical schools in the entire nation.

His grades were quite good. His other qualities, from leadership to extracurricular activities on the campus, were exemplary. He had every reason to believe he would be admitted to medical school.

That is, until the final interview.

The doctor conducting the final phase of admittance studiously poured over Jeff's application. He said very little. Finally, he looked up and said, "I see you attended the University of North Carolina at Chapel Hill."

Jeff nodded. There was another pause as the doctor continued to glance over the application.

Finally, the doctor said, "You need to know that I hate the University of North Carolina. No, that's not strong enough. I despise the University of North Carolina. I attended Duke, and I can't stand UNC."

Jeff waited a few seconds to see if this was simply another joke about an intense rivalry between two very fine institutions, or something more.

He quickly discerned it was something more. He gulped and began to sweat a bit. He thought to himself, "Am I going to be denied admittance because I went to UNC?"

The doctor continued, "In fact, I don't think I've ever met anyone from the University of North Carolina whom I like and respect. And that encompasses almost thirty years since I left Duke!"

"Well," he continued, "let me take that back. There is one person I observed and one day met whom I ended up liking and respecting. He played basketball at the University of North Carolina. When he played, I thought he played with character and enthusiasm. He seemed to be different from the other athletes I observed. Then, one day, he came to Durham, and I had the opportunity to meet him. I wanted to find a way to dislike him. I looked for some reason to find him distasteful. After all, he was a Tar Heel. But I couldn't find anything. I left that encounter with the same respect I felt before meeting him."

Another pause occurred. Finally, he said, "His name was David Chadwick."

Jeff's eyes widened in amazement. He started to speak, then stammered. Finally the words poured out.

"Sir," he said, "David is my mother's first cousin. My mom's dad and David's dad are brothers!"

The doctor was stunned. He looked again at Jeff's application. There it was, as plain as day. He had missed it when he first scanned Jeff's admission form. Jeff Chadwick Wood.

Jeff soon received his letter of acceptance.

Let me state two truths very clearly at this point. First, I don't think I'm that great a guy. I have foibles that could fill my next book! I am very aware of my shortcomings and inadequacies. There are things I did and ways I acted in college that, if I could change, I would do differently. Moreover, I don't remember ever meeting this person. Perhaps I was playing a pickup basketball game there. We often did that against the Duke players. Maybe it was a postseason barnstorming game played at a local high school.

Second, Jeff earned his admission to medical school himself. Moreover, it's very hard for me to believe that a professor would deny Jeff's admission based on his undergraduate university. Surely this doctor had his tongue in his cheek.

However, it does make me feel warm inside that something Dad taught me has proved to be true once again. He told me always to treat people respectfully and rightly. I've tried to do this. He taught me that when I do this, I might never know the impact it has on my life or someone else's.

Although Jeff entered that medical school on his own merits, I would like to think my life, in some small way, helped him.

I haven't practiced this life lesson from Dad because I wanted the future reward. I did it because it is the correct thing to do.

I'm glad it helped Jeff.

I hope it helps my own kids one day.

And I hope it helps anyone else who has been touched by my life.

Part Five

Faith

"I just knew he loved me."

I was only around six years old. Dad was speaking in Mint Hill, North Carolina, a small community just outside of Charlotte. I remember it was dark when we got on the road after Dad had finished speaking. We had not been in the car for more than an hour.

We were driving on a poorly lit, two lane road. We were going the speed limit. Dad had put me in the front seat between himself and Mom. I was barely paying attention as we drove along.

He came out of nowhere. He was unsteady as he walked by the side of the road. Suddenly, he took a step in the street. There was no way Dad could avoid hitting him. He tried to stop. The brakes screeched and the car swerved.

I vividly remember the thud of the car hitting his body. He headed skyward about five feet in the air, then came down. He fell on top of the hood, slid to the windshield, and then fell to the ground on the passenger's side. Then there was silence.

Mom tried to hide my eyes, but I had seen it all. Dad immediately got out of the car. Mom eventually did so, too. I followed. On the ground lay a lifeless body.

The ambulance arrived fairly soon thereafter. The man's body was wheeled away. Later we heard he had died at the scene of the accident.

The coroner's report established that the man was heavily inebriated. That's why he staggered in front of the car. Dad was not responsible.

But I watched Dad grieve. He had killed a man. Yes, it was an accident. But he had killed a man. It haunted his heart.

The next weeks were not easy. Dad had to meet with lawyers and police. Accident reports were filled out. Again, Dad was exonerated. But it was very painful.

Dad knew what he had to do. His lawyer counseled against it. But he had to do it. I guess his pastoral instincts kicked in.

He went to the home of the accident victim. They were icily polite. He didn't admit guilt—there was none to admit. He did express his sorrow. He tried to be compassionate. He told me he put himself in their position and finally concluded that some kind of face-to-face encounter would be helpful. Evidently it was. They felt his sincerity.

I'm convinced it was not only for them he went, but also for himself. He was different when he returned. Something had been taken off his chest. A weight had been lifted.

Later, he told me that he had experienced God's enormous love. "I just knew he loved me," he said.

He had experienced God's love. He knew God's presence. He was able to release the pain and put it in God's palm. God's peace showered his soul.

Dad once told me that while studying philosophy at Duke Divinity School, he discovered a significant truth in his faith pilgrimage. For years, he had engaged himself in academic pursuits. He studied different philosophers and knew they were all seeking the same thing, to understand life and its purpose.

Then he made his discovery. Life's purpose is not found in what you know, but whom you know. Dad found real meaning and purpose in life when he knew God loved him but also when he knew this God of love wanted an intimate, personal relationship with him. That's the God Jesus revealed to him. God became Dad's own heavenly Father.

This is the God he helped me come to know and love.

Someone once said, "You'll never know God is all you need until God is all you've got."

During those dark weeks after the accident, Dad spent a lot of time with God and experienced his profound presence.

It was all he had.

It was all he needed.

"I can still see her dancing around the room."

■

This book is about my dad. It's also meant to promote the incredibly strong influence dads have on their children. That's what my dad has meant to me. I wish Dad could be everyone's dad.

Since that's not possible, I'm writing this book. Lessons he taught me can now be shared with all dads everywhere!

However, I would be remiss if I dismissed the importance of moms. I have a great mom, too. She is equally important in my life and faith development. It's sad to watch her slowly forget more and more. But I'll never forget what she has meant to me!

Neither will Dad forget his own mom. He remembers his parents on their knees at night praying for their kids. It's one of Dad's most powerful memories. I, too, can remember times I saw Mom and Dad on their knees, beseeching Almighty God to care for their children. They did this especially when Howard was in his wilderness wanderings. There's probably no greater power than a dad on his knees, unless it's a mom on her knees.

It was Dad's mom who was the true spiritual force in his family. She led daily Bible studies and Scripture readings. She made sure her two boys were in church every Sunday. Dad also remembers the moments he would see her on her knees, pleading with God that her sons would be committed to him. Her greatest desire was that both boys' lives would be used to help others come to a personal faith in the living Lord Jesus.

And in fact, both became ministers.

But Dad shares that his most vivid picture of his mom is the times he would see her dancing around the room, singing hymns at the top of her voice. They called it her "happy time." She was simply experiencing the joy of the Lord in her heart. Times were tough. The Depression was real. Money was scarce. But even in her tribulations she regularly experienced God's joy.

Obviously, this picture greatly affected Dad and his faith development. To this day, he would say her vibrant, real, joyful faith is what most profoundly touched and developed his own.

You can therefore imagine the trauma involved when my dad, a twelve-year old boy, came to the top of the stairs and saw his own father weeping uncontrollably. Dad's mother had just died. It was rather quick. It could have been cured if penicillin had been on the market. Now, she was gone.

Dad said it took months, perhaps even years, for the grief to subside. It finally did. He rested in the belief that he would see her again.

He also rested in the wonderful, warm memories that flooded his soul.

Particularly, he remembered one picture—her dancing around the room, singing hymns.

That picture will never leave him, even in his eighties.

"Heavenly sunshine . . ."

"'Tis so sweet to trust in Jesus . . ."

"He keeps me singing . . ."

He told me so.

I hope God allows me to see that picture one day in heaven.

"God always tests a calling."

G od gifted Dad with an absolutely beautiful singing voice. Throughout his life, his voice has thrilled all who have had the pleasure of hearing it.

Indeed, his life has always been a balance of music and ministry. When he was a teenager, he attended a Bible camp. He sensed God's call into ministry. He met some men in ministry who helped convince him this was indeed where God was calling him.

Yet he always loved to sing. It was a passion.

Early in his ministry, a public opportunity to sing came his way. Little did he know that a member of the listening audience had connections on Broadway. As with others, he, too, loved Dad's singing voice.

He met with Dad and shared the potential he felt Dad had in New York City. He shared the fame that could be his. He shared how much money Dad could make, ten thousand dollars a year in 1945, compared to Dad's annual salary of fifteen hundred dollars!

Dad was forced to reconsider his call. He looked at all these opportunities that the ministry could never afford him. The temptation to use this extraordinary singing gift on Broadway was before him. In terms of worldly success, it was a simple decision.

But he turned it down. He had felt God's call upon his life. He had a wife and family. As a singer, he envisioned spending long weeks on road trips while his beloved wife and baby stayed home, cramped in a small New York apartment. Instead, he was committed to raising his family in an environment that supported his values and to making his life and gifts glorify God.

Fame, success, and money were rejected. I later asked Dad what he thought was going on. God had called him into the ministry. Why in the world would God allow this temptation to come?

Again, I'll always remember his answer.

"Sometimes," he said, "after God gives a vision, he will test the vision. It's his way of allowing us always to be sure of our calling. In any life, if one is walking with God, there will be a sense of calling. If you desperately desire to do the will of God, God will show you his path. Then comes the temptation. But after you've wrestled with the temptation, you'll never doubt again the path to which you've been called."

He's right. Many people tell me how, after they have made a huge life decision based on what they believe to be God's will for their lives, another opportunity will immediately come their way. They are then forced to revisit the decision they've made. They accept a job and another opportunity comes. They decide to marry a girl, and an old girlfriend calls.

God is sovereign. He is in control. But God never wants us to doubt the direction we're heading. That's why he often challenges a calling.

He did so with Dad. Dad never doubted his ministry calling again.

By the way, Dad's musical gift and singing voice were invaluable in his ministry. He often used them as a part of his messages. Indeed, he recently preached for me and sang, during his sermon, a portion of "The Impossible Dream" from *Man of La Mancha*.

It's almost as if God gave him the best of both worlds, within the parameters of God's desired calling for Dad.

That sounds like a loving Father in heaven to me!

*"God never looks at who you are,
but who you can become."*

D on Quixote, the major character in the play *Man of La Mancha*, is a God-like figure for Dad.

Dad sees this primarily in Don Quixote's relationship with Aldonza, a bar wench he encounters one evening at dinner. When they meet, Don Quixote keeps calling her his Dulcinea. She thinks he's crazy. She is a prostitute. Her past is checkered. Her sin is profound.

Yet Don Quixote keeps calling her his Dulcinea. He sings how he has dreamed about her, the love of his life. He sees her as a beautiful, gifted woman with extraordinary potential. She sees herself as a prostitute whom men use only for their own selfish gratification.

In the last scene in the movie, Don Quixote is lying on his deathbed. A beautiful woman enters. He cannot recognize her. She keeps asking, "Don't you know who I am?" He cannot identify her.

Finally, she tells him. "I am your Dulcinea."

She has become the woman Don Quixote dreamed her to be.

This was a huge part of Dad's theological conviction. He sincerely believed God never saw us as who we were, but who we could become.

Dad would point to Jesus' encounter with Simon Peter. Before he met Jesus, Simon was wishy-washy, had extreme emotions, and was unstable and unreliable. But Jesus immediately named him Peter, the "Rock," the stable one. He saw within Peter potential for greatness. He saw how, when the power of God entered his heart, his self-esteem would be transformed.

Interestingly, Peter did fulfill Jesus' expectation.

At different times in my life, when I have been ready to give up, Dad has always pointed out, "Don't look at the problems, Son, but the possibilities. God is at work. He is doing something. He won't desert you. You have great potential. Believe in yourself. Keep moving forward. God will get you to his destination for your life. You'll find potential you never imagined."

This kind of faith probably allowed a gawky kid from outside of Winston-Salem, North Carolina, to dream his impossible dream. It's probably what allowed my dad to battle through the death of his mother and the poverty of the Depression to become the great man he is today.

It's partly what's motivating me to tell you about him on these pages.

So you, too, can become the person God created you to become.

"Faith is not taught but caught."

▪

Faith was simply a part of my home. It permeated who we were and how we lived.

As early as I can remember, we tried as a family to have a devotional around the dinner table after everyone had finished eating. We were always taken to church. That was simply a normal part of our lives. I can remember seeing both Mom and Dad kneeling beside their bed, asking God for help in times of need. I especially remember these intense, fervent prayers during Howard's time of wandering.

Interestingly, I don't remember times when we deeply studied the Bible together. I don't remember memorizing Bible verses. Although I know these things happened, I don't remember them.

What I do remember is a man who loved God. What I remember is a man caring for the sick and needy. What I remember is a man who helped build an organization to care for the poor and hungry.

I simply remember a man of faith who walked his talk.

During my three years in Europe, I was completely on my own. I wasn't a preacher's kid. I wasn't known by anyone for anything particular. I was just a basketball player living abroad.

These three years alone were valuable for me because they afforded me an opportunity to ask, "Who am I? What do I really believe?"

In essence, I was the perfect Christian athlete while at the University of North Carolina. I traveled the state and gave Christian talks. I had an article written about me in Billy Graham's *Decision* magazine. The Fellowship of Christian Athletes magazine *Sharing the VICTORY* did an article, as did Campus Crusade for Christ's magazine called *Athletes in Action* (a front cover story no less!).

But I had to discover something very important. Did I advocate the Christian faith because I really believed it or because Dad believed it?

My admiration for Dad has existed for as long as I can remember. Therefore, I had to decide if my faith was my own or his.

My time in Europe was not exactly exemplary for a Christian. My last two years were spent on the French Riviera, in Nice, France. My friends tease me and say I needed to go to seminary to make up for the two years spent as a bachelor on the French Riviera!

I eventually found my answer. It was partly during my European adventure. It was partly in the rejection I received from the girl in South Florida.

But I finally found it. My belief is my own!

God became personal for me.

However, I'd be terribly remiss if I didn't say Dad's faith hasn't profoundly affected me. It has.

I've learned much through his words. His sermons are deep, biblical, and thoughtful. Our one-on-one times, to this day, are highlights. He always gives me insights about faith.

But the primary reason I believe is because I see him live his belief. It is so very real to him. It has become real to me.

"Son," he once said to me, "faith is caught, not taught."

And I caught it.

Through Dad . . . to God!

"Adversity is life's university."

■

Ever had one of those times when everything you touched turned to trash? Even when you think you've done the proper preparation, received the proper counsel, presented the proper way, it still turned sour?

That happened to me in the early 90s. To this day, I can't explain it. I was trying to implement a new strategy in the church. I was absolutely certain it was what we needed to do. I had done the planning and had run it by my leadership. I was certain I had presented it in the most vibrant, enthusiastic way possible. Buyin was there. We began the work and it failed miserably. I tried to reimplement the plan. I tried even harder. Once again, it was ppppffffffffffttttttt—the air going out of the balloon, me spinning around, bouncing off walls like that balloon, and then failure. I scratched my head in disbelief. I couldn't figure it out. Nothing I did succeeded!

It almost felt as if God was looking down on me and saying, "Nope, that is not going to work. No matter how hard you try to make it succeed, it won't. Nope, that won't work either. You can keep trying, but it's going to fail."

In total exasperation, I went to Dad. Not only was I frustrated with the implementation of this plan, I was frustrated with ministry! Frankly, I was sick and tired of it all.

I told him the story and my feelings. He simply shrugged and said, "Son, don't you know by now that adversity is life's university?" Then he shared with me the reality that every defeat is simply an opportunity to learn. Indeed when I told him what I thought God might be doing, he responded, "Maybe he is. I have no doubt that sometimes in our lives God purposefully and intentionally frustrates our plans so we can learn a larger lesson. Maybe God is trying to teach you patience? Or perseverance? Or hope? God knows, and it's your job to find out."

"After all," he concluded, "man proposes but God disposes."

Oh my, there's another one of those sayings. I haven't forgotten that one either!

I knew Dad was right, and the years since this experience have increasingly shown me his wisdom. God is using everything, somehow, some way, for his purposes. That's what faith is, believing—especially when it doesn't make sense.

It reminds me of an experience I recently had. I was at WBT radio recording my program. After my first guest, I had a break because my producer had to attend to some problem. I took a stretch in the halls and heard a familiar voice around the corner. I followed the sounds only to walk in on the inimitable Mr. T, of *Rocky*-movie and A *Team*-television fame.

"Who are you, fool?" he asked me.

"I am a local pastor who does a weekly radio program about faith and values intersecting contemporary issues," I responded.

Then a brainstorm hit me. Knowing Mr. T was a Christian (I'd read it somewhere), I blurted out, "You want to be on my program?"

He didn't flinch. "Let's go, fool," he said.

We went into the studio. He stood in front of the mike. I asked him one question. "Tell me about your faith and what God has taught you about life."

He began by sharing about his experience with cancer, which threatened his life in 1995. He talked about how God had walked with him through the experience. He shared the pain, trial, and turmoil as he wondered if he would live. Now, on the other side, he said he was a richer human being because of the adversity.

Then he said something I'll never forget. "Always remember this, 'No test, no testimony!' Always remember that, all you fools out there listening to me. No test, no testimony."

Adversity is life's university. Man proposes; God disposes. No test, no testimony. Take your pick. Two are from my Dad. One from Mr. T.

But they all say the same thing.

And it's a lesson we all need to learn.

*"My God, in all his loving kindness,
has met me at every corner."*

■

This is Dad's life verse. It's a paraphrase of Psalm 59:10, and Dad loves to quote it. It describes his life and faith. From his childhood to his eighties, Dad believes God is always present, always helping, his personal Friend. He believes his sins have been forgiven, and the friendship is secure.

This friendship guided him through the death of his mom at the impressionable age of twelve and through his teenage years as he and his family confronted the hard times of the Depression.

This friendship guided him through seminary and marriage. God was on the train with him when he was wrestling with whether or not to leave the Moravian denomination and join the Presbyterian one. While riding home, he read a devotional that simply said, "Yield yourself to the highest in the kingdom of God." He knew God's voice had spoken. He slept like a baby for the first time in weeks.

He entrusted his three children to this Friend, even when they were wandering, even when they were behaving in a way that he knew didn't reflect his values and convictions. He knew they were actually his Friend's children, on loan for a few years this side of eternity. Therefore, he could trust the Friend to take care of his own possessions.

This friendship guided him through interpersonal and church crises, when his very future was uncertain, when he wondered why supposed friends would treat him as they did. The Friend gave him the power to forgive and to use the pain for eternal good.

This friendship guided him through new adventures, during years of supposed retirement to even greener fields of ministry. The Friend had promised he would take care of Dad. He kept his promise in abundance.

This friendship guides him now, in his eighties, as he cares for the woman he loves who cannot remember what happened five minutes ago, during the times when he longs for adult conversation with her, and in the midst of memories of their happy years. Yet he continues to love because his Friend gives him the strength to love. He has come to the conclusion that his Friend is much more concerned about their eternal friendship than present comfort. Slowly but surely, Dad is acting more and more like his Friend, desiring to serve and not be served, to give and not always receive. The Friend has told him that's a part of the outcome of what Mom is going through.

The Friend really loves my dad. Therefore, he is continually guiding my dad, meeting him, and preparing him every day for his real home.

I recently asked Dad if he was afraid to die. He laughed.

"No, not at all," he answered. "Why should I be afraid? My Friend has met me at every corner. He always has. He always will."

This explains the title of the book.

Dad knows with certainty two truths about God. First, God is his faithful, eternal Father. Second, God is Dad's close, caring Friend. God is his Father, his Friend. That's who Dad is to me. My father; my friend. And God is *my* Father and Friend because Dad showed me this truth through his relationship with me.

My prayer is that this little book helps you know my dad. He is a wonderful dad. I wish he could be everyone's dad.

Further, my prayer is that this little book helps you know Dad's Friend. That's what Dad would want, too. All Dad is and has is because of this Friend.

He is real. He is alive.

His name is Jesus.

If you don't believe me, ask Dad.

He'd be more than happy to tell you in whom he believes.

"We know who waits for us on the other side."

I know Dad, in his eighties, has thought about death. I therefore recently broached the subject with him.

"Dad," I asked, "What do you think death will be like?"

He paused for a moment. Then he said, "Son, I rather think death will be like two babies in a womb. They are talking to one another, uncertain what life outside the womb will be like. At times, they experience some fear of the unknown. But if they only knew that on the other side were waiting the loving hands of their mom and dad, plus all the dozens of other people who will immediately love them, they wouldn't fear at all. Indeed, they would be excited about entering this new world."

"Well," he concluded, "that's what I think death is like. We're here, talking about it. There's some fear of the unknown. The difference is we *know* there is One on the other side, lovingly and graciously waiting for us. We *know* there are many others, what the Bible calls 'a cloud of witnesses,' waiting for us. Therefore, I'll miss you and our family, but I'll be excited to see and be with all those who lovingly and graciously await me, especially my Lord and Savior.

"I'll receive my resurrection body, no more pain, tears, turmoil . . . and Alzheimer's!"

Probably the fact that there will be no more Alzheimer's is, at this moment, Dad's greatest resurrection hope. But rest assured, he is not afraid of death.

He knows who waits for him on the other side.

"In you, Dad, I see the face of God my eternal Father."

O bviously, Dad didn't say the words quoted above. I did and have . . . many, many times.

I believe one of God's major means of grace is the experience of the heavenly Father's love through an earthly daddy's love. That's why Jesus helped teach us about God by calling him "Abba," an Aramaic colloquialism that means "Daddy." When a father would come home from work, it was the phrase his child would utter as she rushed into his arms.

Through the words of my father, I've learned about life and faith. And that faith has been the most important part of my life's pilgrimage.

But I learned about faith not only from Dad's words; I learned by seeing it in his face. I see it when he sings about his Father in heaven. I see it when he prays at the table. I see it when he speaks from the pulpit. I see it when he hugs me. I see it when he loves a woman with dementia.

When I was a little boy, I slept in a room where Mom had placed a laundry can. It was about four feet high and ten inches wide, a perfect cylinder that stood at the bedroom door.

At night, I saw a shadow of that cylinder. At the top were a few curves that made the shadow look like the face of a man. When I first noticed it, my heart leapt in fear. I imagined an evil, shadowy figure that wanted to do me harm. For several nights, it was difficult to go to sleep.

Until one night, the problem was solved. While staring at it, I looked at all the curves and concluded the face was the face of my dad. He wasn't sinister, but caring. It wasn't evil, but loving.

I fell asleep and never feared the evil shadow again.

Through the years, with his words and face, Dad has taught me that in every shadow I can see the face of my Father in heaven. No matter what may happen to me—severe rejections, disappointments, near-death experiences, frustrations with people—my Daddy in heaven, my closest Friend, is with me in the shadows. He is working through them for good. I can trust him. I don't need to fear or worry.

I can see the face of my Father who is my Friend in heaven in the shadows.

That is all I need to know.

Epilogue

Epilogue

■

The Bible says that when we were young, we thought like children. That certainly was the case with me.

Whenever Dad would come home from a trip, I would be very excited to see him. I would bound to the door, hug him, and then ask the inevitable question, "Did you bring me some presents?" As a child, the relationship was largely dependent on what he brought me, the presents he bought me.

Now that I am an adult, I have a completely different relationship with him. When I am with him, I could care less about presents. I don't want anything from him. I just want to be with him.

There is a parallel here also with our faith. An immature faith is always asking for gifts from God. When we pray, the dominant theme is our grocery list of wants and supposed needs. The proof of the relationship is how many items on this list God gives us. If he doesn't come through, he is faithless, and we're in despair. If he does come through, then we worship and adore him.

What an immature faith! God is worthy of praise and adoration simply because he is. He has already given us much more than we deserve. Just look around! But even if all we had was one instant on this side of creation, that would be enough to give God his just honor and due.

To love God has little to do with his presents to us, which are abundant. Our love for God has much more to do with simply being in a personal, eternal relationship with him, simply enjoying His presence.

A few minutes now with an incredibly wise man in his eighties are a far greater pleasure than any gifts I received from him in my earlier years.

Yet another valuable lesson you taught me, Dad.

I hope God gives us a few more good years together so I can continue in your presence.

If so, what a gift!

If not, see you in heaven!